Selected Prefaces
and Introductions of
W. Somerset Maugham

Selected Prefaces
and Introductions of
W. Somerset Maugham

Doubleday & Company, Inc.

Garden City, New York

1963

Publisher's Note

By Mr. Maugham's direction a few passages have been deleted to eliminate repetition or references that might be confusing today unless the reader had at hand the works to which the Prefaces and Introductions apply.

Contents

* Though this essay appeared in the book as Chapter One it is essentially an Introduction and so is here included.

Part I

CONCERNING
MR. MAUGHAM'S OWN WORKS

From:

The Art of Fiction

"Chapter One"*
(1948–1955)

I should like to tell the reader of this book how the essays in it first came to be written. One day, while I was in the United States, the Editor of *Redbook* asked me to make a list of what in my opinion were the ten best novels in the world. I did so, and thought no more about it. Of course my list was arbitrary. I could have made one of ten other novels, just as good in their different ways as those I chose, and given just as sound reasons for selecting them. If a hundred persons, well read and of adequate culture, were asked to produce such a list, in all probability at least two or three hundred novels would be mentioned, but I think that in all the lists most of those I have chosen would find a place. That there should be a diversity of opinion in this matter is understandable. There are various reasons that make a particular novel so much appeal to a person, even of sound judgment, that he is led to ascribe outstanding merit to it. It may be that he has read it at a time of life when, or in circumstances in which, he was peculiarly liable to be moved by it; or it may be that its theme, or its setting, has a more than ordinary significance for him owing to his own predilections or personal associations. I can imagine that a passionate lover of music might place Henry Handel Richardson's *Maurice*

---

* Though this essay appeared in the book as Chapter One it is essentially an Introduction and so is here included.

Guest among the ten best novels, and a native of the Five Towns, delighted with the fidelity with which Arnold Bennett described their character and their inhabitants, might in his list place *The Old Wives' Tale*. Both are good novels, but I do not think an unbiassed judgment would put either of them among the best ten. The nationality of a reader lends to certain works an interest that inclines him to attribute a greater excellence to them than would generally be admitted. During the eighteenth century, English literature was widely read in France, but since then, till fairly recently, the French have not taken much interest in anything that was written beyond their own frontiers, and I don't suppose it would occur to a Frenchman to mention *Moby Dick* in such a list as I myself made, and *Pride and Prejudice* only if he were of quite unusual culture; he would certainly, however, include Madame de Lafayette's *La Princesse de Clèves;* and rightly, for it has outstanding merits. It is a novel of sentiment, a psychological novel, perhaps the first that was ever written: the story is touching; the characters are soundly drawn; it is written with distinction, and it is commendably brief. It deals with a state of society which is well known to every schoolboy in France; its moral atmosphere is familiar to him from his reading of Corneille and Racine; it has the glamour of association with the most splendid period of French history, and it is a worthy contribution to the golden age of French literature. But the English reader may think the magnanimity of the protagonists inhuman, their discourse with one another stilted, and their behaviour incredible. I do not say he is right to think this; but thinking it, he will never class this admirable novel among the ten best in the world.

In a brief commentary to accompany the list of books I made for *Redbook*, I wrote: "The wise reader will get the greatest enjoyment out of reading them if he learns the useful art of skipping." A sensible person does not read a novel as a task. He reads it as a diversion. He is prepared to interest himself in the characters and is concerned to see how they act in given circumstances, and what happens to them; he sympathizes with their troubles and is gladdened by their joys; he puts himself in their place and, to an extent, lives their lives. Their view of life, their attitude to the great subjects of human speculation, whether stated in words or shown in action, call forth in him a reaction of surprise, of pleasure or of indignation. But he knows instinctively where his interest lies and he follows it as surely as a hound follows the scent of a fox. Sometimes, through the author's failure, he loses the scent. Then he flounders about till he finds it again. He skips.

Everybody skips, but to skip without loss is not easy. It may be, for all I know, a gift of nature, or it may be something that has to be acquired by experience. Dr. Johnson skipped ferociously, and Boswell tells us that "he had a peculiar facility in seizing at once what was valuable in any book without submitting to the labour of perusing it from beginning to end." Boswell was doubtless referring to books of information or of edification; if it is a labour to read a novel it is better not to read it at all. Unfortunately, for reasons I shall go into presently, there are few novels which it is possible to read from beginning to end with unfailing interest. Though skipping may be a bad habit, it is one that is forced upon the reader. But when the reader once begins to skip, he finds it hard to stop, and so may miss much that it would have been to his advantage to read.

Now it so happened that some time after the list I had made for *Redbook* appeared, an American publisher put before me the suggestion of reissuing the ten novels I had mentioned in an abridged form, with a preface to each one written by me. His idea was to omit everything but what told the story the author had to tell, expose his relevant ideas and display the characters he had created so that readers might read these fine novels, which they would not have done unless what might not unfairly be described as a lot of dead wood had been cut away from them; and thus, since nothing but what was valuable was left in them, enjoy to the full a great intellectual pleasure. I was at first taken aback; but then I reflected that though some of us have acquired the knack of skipping to our profit, most people have not, and it would surely be a good thing if they could have their skipping done for them by a person of tact and discrimination. I welcomed the notion of writing the prefaces to the novels in question, and presently set to work. Some students of literature, some professors and critics, will exclaim that it is a shocking thing to mutilate a masterpiece, and that it should be read as the author wrote it. That depends on the masterpiece. I cannot think that a single page could be omitted from so enchanting a novel as *Pride and Prejudice,* or from one so tightly constructed as *Madame Bovary;* but that very sensible critic George Saintsbury wrote that "there is very little fiction that will stand concentration and condensation as well as that of Dickens." There is nothing reprehensible in cutting. Few plays have ever been produced that were not to their advantage more or less drastically cut in rehearsal. One day, many years ago, when we were lunching together, Bernard Shaw told me that his plays were much more successful in Germany than they were in England. He ascribed this to the stupidity of the British public and to the greater intelligence of the German. He was wrong. In England he insisted that every word he had written should be spoken. I had seen his plays in Germany; there the directors had ruthlessly pruned them of verbiage unnecessary to the dramatic action, and so provided the public with an entertainment that was thoroughly enjoyable. I did not, however, think it well to tell him this. I know no reason why a novel should not be subjected to a similar process.

Coleridge said of *Don Quixote* that it is a book to read through once and then only to dip into, by which he may well have meant that parts of it are so tedious, and even absurd, that it is time illspent, when you have once dis-

covered this, to read them again. It is a great and important
book, and a professed student of literature should certainly
read it once through (I have myself read it from cover to
cover twice in English and three times in Spanish), yet I cannot but think that the ordinary reader, the reader who reads
for delight, would lose nothing if he did not read the dull
parts at all. He would surely enjoy all the more the passages
in which the narrative is directly concerned with the adventures and conversations, so amusing and so touching, of the
gentle knight and his earthly squire. A Spanish publisher has,
in point of fact, collected these in a single volume. It makes
very good reading. There is another novel, certainly important, but to be called great only with hesitation, Samuel
Richardson's *Clarissa*, which is of a length to defeat all but
the most obstinate of novel readers. I do not believe I could
ever have brought myself to read it if I had not come across
a copy in an abridged form. The abridgment had been so well
done that I had no feeling that anything was lost.

I suppose most people would admit that Marcel Proust's
À la Recherche du Temps Perdu is the greatest novel that
has been produced in this century. Proust's fanatical admirers, of whom I am one, can read every word of it with interest; in a moment of extravagance, I stated once that I would
sooner be bored by Proust than amused by any other writer;
but I am prepared now, after a third reading, to admit that
the various parts of his book are of unequal merit. I suspect
that the future will cease to be interested in those long sec-
tions of desultory reflection which Proust wrote under the
influence of ideas current in his day, but now in part discarded and in part commonplace. I think then it will be more
evident than it is now that he was a great humourist and that
his power to create characters, original, various and lifelike,
places him on an equality with Balzac, Dickens and Tolstoy.
It may be that some day an abridged version of his immense work will be issued from which will be omitted those
passages that time has stripped of their value and only those

retained which, because they are of the essence of a novel, remain of enduring interest. À la Recherche du Temps Perdu will still be a very long novel, but it will be a superb one. So far as I can make out from the somewhat complicated account in André Maurois' admirable book, À la Recherche de Marcel Proust, the author's intention was to publish his novel in three volumes of about four hundred pages each. The second and third volumes were in print when the First World War broke out, and publication was postponed. Proust's health was too poor to allow him to serve in the war and he used the ample leisure thus at his disposal to add to the third volume an immense amount of material. "Many of the additions," says Maurois, "are psychological and philosophical dissertations, in which the intelligence" (by which I take him to mean the author in person) "comments on the actions of the characters." And he adds: "One could compile from them a series of essays after the manner of Montaigne; on the role of music, novelty in the arts, beauty of style, on the small number of human types, on flair in medicine, etc." That is true, but whether they add to the value of the novel as a novel depends, I suppose, on what opinions you hold on the essential function of the form.

On this different people have different opinions. H. G. Wells wrote an interesting essay which he called The Contemporary Novel: "So far as I can see," he says, "it is the only medium through which we can discuss the great majority of the problems which are being raised in such a bristling multitude by our contemporary social development." The novel of the future "is to be the social mediator, the vehicle of understanding, the instrument of self-examination, the parade of morals and the exchange of manners, the factory of customs, the criticism of laws and institutions and of social dogmas and ideas." "We are going to deal with political questions and religious questions." Wells had little patience with the idea that it was merely a means of relaxation, and he stated categorically that he could not bring himself to look upon it as an art-form. Strangely enough, he resented having his own novels described as propaganda, "because it seems to me that the word propaganda should be confined to the definite service of some organised party, church or doctrine." The word, at all events now, has a larger meaning than that; it indicates the method through which by word of mouth, through the written word, by advertisement, by constant repetition, you seek to persuade others that your views of what is right and proper, good and bad, just and unjust, are the correct views, and should be accepted and acted upon by all and sundry. Wells's principal novels were designed to diffuse certain doctrines and principles; and that is propaganda.

What it all comes down to is the question whether the novel is a form of art or not. Is its aim to instruct or to please? If its aim is to instruct, then it is not a form of art. For the aim of art is to please. On this poets, painters and philosophers are agreed. But it is a truth that shocks a good many people, since Christianity has taught them to look upon pleasure with misgiving as a snare to entangle the immortal soul. It seems more reasonable to look upon pleasure as a good, but to remember that certain pleasures have mischievous consequence and so may more wisely be eschewed. There is a general disposition to look upon pleasure as merely sensual, and that is natural since the sensual pleasures are more vivid than the intellectual; but that is surely an error, for there are pleasures of the mind as well as of the body, and if they are not so keen, they are more enduring. The Oxford Dictionary gives as one of the meanings of art: "The application of skill to subjects of taste, as poetry, music, dancing, the drama, oratory, literary composition, and the like." That is very well, but then it adds: "Especially in modern use skill displaying itself in perfection of workmanship, perfection of execution as an object in itself." I suppose that is what every novelist aims at, but as we know, he never achieves it. I think we may claim that the novel is a form of art, perhaps not a very exalted one, but a form of art nevertheless. It is, however, an essentially imperfect form. Since I have dealt with this subject in lectures which I have delivered here and there, and can put what I have to say now no better than I did in them, I am going to permit myself briefly to quote from them.

I think it an abuse to use the novel as a pulpit or a platform, and I believe readers are misguided when they suppose they can thus easily acquire knowledge. It is a great nuisance that knowledge can only be acquired by hard work. It would be fine if we could swallow the powder of profitable information made palatable by the jam of fiction. But the truth is that, so made palatable, we can't be sure that the powder will be profitable, for the knowledge the novelist imparts is biassed and thus unreliable; and it is better not to know a thing at all than to know it in a distorted fashion. There is no reason why a novelist should be anything but a novelist. It is enough if he is a good novelist. He should know a little about a great many things, but it is unnecessary, and sometimes even harmful, for him to be a specialist in any particular subject. He need not eat a whole sheep to know what mutton tastes like; it is enough if he eats a chop. Then, by applying his imagination and his creative faculty to the chop he has eaten, he can give you a pretty good idea of an Irish Stew; but when he goes on from this to broach his views on sheepraising, the wool industry and the political situation in Australia, it is wise to accept them with reserve.

The novelist is at the mercy of his bias. The subjects he chooses, the characters he invents and his attitude towards them, are conditioned by it. Whatever he writes is the expression of his personality and it is the manifestation of his innate instincts, his feelings and his experience. However hard he tries to be objective, he remains the slave of his idiosyncrasies. However hard he tries to be impartial, he cannot help taking sides. He loads his dice. By the mere fact of introducing a character to your notice early in his novel, he enlists your interest and your sympathy in that character. Henry James insisted again and again that the novelist must dramatize. That is a telling, though perhaps not very lucid, way of saying that he must arrange his facts in such a manner as to capture and hold your attention. So, if need be, he will sacrifice verisimilitude and credibility to the effect he wants to get. That, as we know, is not the way a work of scientific or informative value is written. The aim of the writer of fiction is not to instruct, but to please.

There are two main ways in which a novel may be written. Each has its advantages, and each its disadvantages. One way is to write it in the first person, and the other is to write it from the standpoint of omniscience. In the latter, the author can tell you all that he thinks is needful to enable you to follow his story and understand his characters. He can describe their emotions and motives from the inside. If one of them crosses the street, he can tell you why he does so and what will come of it. He can concern himself with one set of persons and series of events, and then, putting them aside for a period, can concern himself with another set of events and another set of persons, so reviving a flagging interest and, by complicating his story, give an impression of the multifariousness, complexity and diversity of life. The danger of this is that one set of characters may be so much more interesting than the other, as, to take a famous example, happens in *Middlemarch,* that the reader may find it irksome when he is asked to occupy himself with the fortunes of persons he doesn't in the least care about. The novel written from the standpoint of omniscience runs the risk of being unwieldy, verbose and diffuse. No one has written it better than Tolstoy, but even he is not free from these imperfections. The method makes demands on the author which he cannot always meet. He has to get into the skin of every one of his characters, feel his feelings, think his thoughts; but he has his limitations and he can only do this when there is in himself something of the character he has created. When there isn't, he can only see him from the outside, and then the character lacks the persuasiveness which causes the reader to believe in him.

I suppose it was because Henry James, with his solicitude for form in the novel, became conscious of these disadvantages that he devised what may be described as a sub-variety of the method of omniscience. In this the author is still omniscient, but his omniscience is concentrated in a single character, and since the character is fallible the omniscience is not complete. The author wraps himself in omniscience when he writes: "He saw her smile"; but not when he writes: "He saw the irony of her smile"; for irony is something he ascribes to her smile, and it may be, without justification. The usefulness of the device, as Henry James without doubt very well saw, is that since this particular character, in *The Ambassadors*, Strether, is all important, and it is through what he sees, hears, feels, thinks, surmises that the story is told, and the characters of the other persons concerned in it are unfolded, the author finds it easy to resist the irrelevant. The construction of his novel is necessarily compact. The device, besides, gives an air of verisimilitude to what he writes. Because you are asked to concern yourself primarily with one person, you are insensibly led to believe what he tells you. The facts that the reader should know are imparted to him as the person through whom the story is told gradually learns them; and so the reader enjoys the pleasure of the elucidation, step by step, of what was puzzling, obscure and uncertain. The method thus gives the novel something of the mystery of a detective story, and so that dramatic quality which Henry James was always eager to obtain. The danger, however, of divulging little by little a string of facts is that the reader may be more quick-witted than the character through whom the revelations are made and so guess the answers long before the author wishes him to. I don't suppose anyone can read *The Ambassadors* without growing impatient with Strether's obtuseness. He does not see what is staring him in the face, and what everyone he comes in contact with is fully aware of. It was a *secret de Polichinelle* and that Strether should not have guessed it points to some defect in the method. It is unsafe to take your reader for more of a fool than he is.

Since novels have for the most part been written from the standpoint of omniscience, it must be supposed that novelists have found it on the whole the most satisfactory way of dealing with their difficulties; but to tell a story in the first person has also certain advantages. Like the method adopted by Henry James, it lends verisimilitude to the narrative and obliges the author to stick to his point; for he can tell you only what he has himself seen, heard or done. To use this method more often would have served the great English novelists of the nineteenth century well, since, partly owing to methods of publication, partly owing to a national idiosyncrasy, their novels have tended to be shapeless and discursive. Another advantage of using the first person is that it enlists your sympathy with the narrator. You may disapprove of him, but he concentrates your attention on himself and so compels your sympathy. A disadvantage of the method, however, is that the narrator, when, as in *David Copperfield*, he is also the hero, cannot without impropriety tell you that he is handsome and attractive; he is apt to seem vainglorious when he relates his doughty deeds and stupid when he fails to see, what is obvious to the reader, that the heroine loves him. But a greater disadvantage still, and one that no authors of this kind of novel have managed entirely to surmount, is that the hero-narrator, the central character, is likely to appear pallid in comparison with the persons he is concerned with. I have asked myself why this should be, and the only explanation I can suggest is that the author, since he sees himself in the hero, sees him from the inside, subjectively, and telling what he sees, gives him the confusions, the weaknesses, the indecisions he feels in himself; whereas he sees the other characters from the outside, objectively, through his imagination and his intuition; and if he is an author with say, Dickens's brilliant gifts, he sees them with a dramatic intensity, with a boisterous sense of fun, with a keen delight in their oddity, and so makes them stand out with a vividness that overshadows his portrait of himself.

There is a variety of the novel written on these lines which for a time had an immense vogue. This is the novel written in letters; each letter, of course, is written in the first person, but the letters are by different hands. The method had the advantage of extreme verisimilitude. The reader might easily believe that they were real letters, written by the persons they purported to have been written by, and come into his hands by a betrayal of confidence. Now, verisimilitude is what the novelist strives to achieve above all else; he wants you to believe that what he tells you actually happened, even if it is improbable as the tales of Baron Munchausen or as horrifying as Kafka's *The Castle*. But the genre had grave defects. It was a roundabout, complicated way of telling a story, and it told it with intolerable deliberation. The letters were too often verbose and contained irrelevant matter. Readers grew bored with the method and it died out. It produced three books which may be accounted among the masterpieces of fiction: *Clarissa*, *La Nouvelle Heloise* and *Les Liaisons Dangereuses*.

There is, however, a variety of the novel written in the first person which, to my mind, avoids the defects of the method and yet makes handsome use of its merits. It is, perhaps, the most convenient and effective way in which a novel can be written. To what good use it can be put may be seen in Herman Melville's *Moby Dick*. In this variety, the author tells the story himself, but he is not the hero and it is not his story that he tells. He is a character in it, and is more or less closely connected with the persons who take part in it. His role is not to determine the action, but to be the confidant, the mediator, the observer of those who do take part in it. Like the chorus in a Greek tragedy, he reflects on the circumstances which he witnesses; he may lament, he may advise, he has no power to influence the course of events. He takes the reader into his confidence, tells him what he knows, hopes or fears, and when he is non-plussed frankly tells him so. There is no need to make him stupid, so that he should not divulge to the reader what the author wishes to hold back, as happens when the story is told through such a character as Henry James's Strether. On the contrary, he can be as keen-witted and clear-sighted as the author can make him. The narrator and the reader are united in their common interest in the persons of the story, their characters, motives and conduct; and the narrator begets in the reader the same sort of familiarity with the creatures of his invention as he has himself. He gets an effect of verisimilitude as persuasive as that which the author obtains who is himself the hero of his novel. He can so build up his protagonist as to arouse your sympathy and show him in an heroic light, which the hero-narrator cannot do without somewhat exciting your antagonism. A method of writing a novel which conduces to the reader's intimacy with the characters, and adds to its verisimilitude, has obviously much to recommend it.

I will venture now to state what in my opinion are the qualities that a good novel should have. It should have a widely interesting theme, by which I mean a theme interesting not only to a clique, whether of critics, professors, highbrows, bus-conductors, or bartenders, but so broadly human that its appeal is to men and women in general; and the theme should be of enduring interest: the novelist is rash who elects to write on subjects of which interest is merely topical. When they cease to be so, his novel will be as unreadable as last week's newspaper. The story the author has to tell should be coherent and persuasive; it should have a beginning, a middle and an end, and the end should be the natural consequence of the beginning. The episodes should have probability and should not only develop the theme, but grow out of the story. The creatures of the novelist's invention should be observed with individuality, and their actions should proceed from their characters; the reader must never be allowed to say: "So and so would never behave like that"; on the contrary, he should be obliged to say: "That's exactly how I should have expected so and so to behave." I think it is all the better if the characters are in themselves interesting. In Flaubert's *L'Education Sentimentale* he wrote a novel which has a great reputation among many excellent critics, but he chose for his hero a man so null, so featureless, so vapid that it is impossible to care what he does or what happens to him; and in consequence, for all its merits, the book is hard to read. I think I should explain why I say that characters should be observed with individuality; it is too much to expect the novelist to create characters that are quite new; his material is human nature, and although there are all sorts and conditions of men, the sorts are not infinite, and novels, stories, plays, epics have been written for so many hundreds of years that the chance is small that an author will create an entirely new character. Casting my mind's eye over the whole of fiction, the only absolutely original creation I can think of is Don Quixote, and I should not be surprised to learn that some learned critic had found a remote ancestry for him also. The author is fortunate if he can see his characters through his own individuality, and if his individuality is sufficiently out of the common to give them an illusive air of originality.

And just as behaviour should proceed from character, so should speech. A woman of fashion should talk like a woman of fashion, a street-walker like a street-walker, a racing tout like a racing tout and an attorney like an attorney. (It is surely a fault in Meredith and Henry James that their characters invariably talk like Henry James and Meredith respectively.) The dialogue should be neither desultory nor should it be an occasion for the author to air his views; it should serve to characterize the speakers and advance the story. The narrative passages should be vivid, to the point, and no longer than is necessary to make the motives of the persons concerned, and the situations in which they are placed, clear and convincing. The writing should be simple enough for anyone of fair education to read with ease, and the manner should fit the matter as a well-cut shoe fits a shapely foot. Finally, a novel should be entertaining. I have put this last, but it is the essential quality, without which no other quality avails. And the more intelligent the entertainment a novel offers, the better it is. Entertainment is a word that has a good many meanings. One item is that which affords interest or amusement. It is a common error to suppose that in this sense amusement is the only one of importance. There is as much entertainment to be obtained from *Wuthering Heights* or *The Brothers Karamazov* as from *Tristram Shandy* or *Candide*. The appeal is different, but equally legitimate. Of course, the novelist has the right to deal with those great topics which are of concern to every human being, the existence of God, the immortality of the soul, the meaning and value of life; though he is prudent to remember that wise saying of Dr. Johnson's that of these topics one can no longer say anything new about them that is true, or anything true about them that is new. The novelist can only hope to interest his reader in what he has to say about them if they are an integral element of the story he has to tell, essential to the characterization of the persons of his novel and affect their conduct—that is, if they result in action which otherwise would not have taken place.

But even if the novel has all the qualities that I have mentioned, and that is asking a lot, there is, like a flaw in a precious stone, a faultiness in the form that renders perfection impossible to attain. That is why no novel is perfect. A short story is a piece of fiction that can be read, according to its length, in anything between ten minutes and an hour, and it deals with a single, well-defined subject, an incident or a closely related series of incidents, spiritual or material, which is complete. It should be impossible to add to it or to take away from it. Here, I believe, perfection can be reached, and I do not think it would be difficult to collect a number of short stories in which this has in fact been done. But a novel is a narrative of indefinite length; it may be as long as *War and Peace*, in which a succession of events is related and a vast number of characters are displayed through a period of time, or as short as *Carmen*. Now, in order to give probability to his story, the author has to narrate a series of facts that are relevant to it, but that are not in themselves interesting. Events often require to be separated by a lapse of time, and the author for the balance of his work has to insert, as best he can, matter that will fill up this lapse. These passages are known as bridges. Most writers resign themselves to crossing them, and they cross them with more or less skill, but it is only too likely that in the process they will be tedious. The novelist is human and it is inevitable that he should be susceptible to the fashions of his day, since after all he has an unusual affectivity, and so is often led to write what, as the fashion passes, loses its attractiveness. Let me give an instance: until the nineteenth century novelists paid little attention to scenery, a word or two sufficed to enable them to say all they wanted to about it; but when the romantic school, and the example of Chateaubriand, captivated the public fancy, it grew modish to write descriptions for their own sake. A man could not go down a street to buy a toothbrush at the chemist's without the author telling you what the houses he passed looked like and what articles were for sale in the shops. Dawn and the setting sun, the starry night, the cloudless sky, the snow-capped mountains, the dark forests—all gave occasion to interminable descriptions. Many were in themselves beautiful; but they were irrelevant: it took writers a long time to discover that a description of scenery, however poetically observed and admirably expressed, was futile unless it was necessary—that is, unless it helped the author to get on with his story or told the reader something it behoved him to know about the persons who take part in it. This is an adventitious imperfection in the novel, but there is yet another that seems inherent. Since it is a work of considerable length, it must take some time to write, weeks at least, generally months and occasionally even years. It is only too likely that the author's inventiveness will sometimes fail him. Then he can only fall back on dogged industry and his general competence. It will be a marvel if by these means he can hold his readers' attention.

In the past, readers, preferring quantity to quality, to get their money's worth wanted their novels long, and the author was often hard put to it to provide more matter for the printer than the story he had to tell required. He hit upon an easy way to do this. He inserted into his novel stories, sometimes long enough to be called novelettes, which had nothing to do with his theme or, at best, were tacked on to it with little plausibility. No writer did this with greater nonchalance than Cervantes in *Don Quixote*. These interpolations have always been regarded as a blot on an immortal work, and can only be read now with impatience. Contemporary criticism attacked him on this account, and in the second part of the book we know he eschewed the bad practice, so producing what is generally thought to be impossible, a sequel that was better than its forerunner; but this did not prevent succeeding writers (who doubtless had not read the criticisms) from using so convenient a device to enable them to deliver to the booksellers a quantity of copy sufficient to make a saleable volume. In the nineteenth century new methods of publication exposed novelists to new temptations. Monthly magazines that devoted much of their space to what is somewhat depreciatingly known as light literature achieved great success, and so provided authors with the opportunity to bring their work before the public in serial form with profit to themselves. At about the same time, the publishers found it to their advantage to issue the novels of popular authors in monthly numbers. The authors contracted to provide a certain amount of material to fill a certain number of pages. The system encouraged them to be leisurely and long-winded. We know from their own admissions how from time to time the authors of these serials, even the best of them, Dickens, Thackeray, Trollope, found it a hateful burden to be obliged to deliver an instalment by a given date. No wonder they padded! No wonder they burdened their stories with irrelevant episodes! When I consider how many obstacles the novelist has to contend with, how many pitfalls to avoid, I am not surprised that even the greatest novels are imperfect; I am only surprised that they are not more imperfect than they are.

I have in my time, hoping to improve myself, read several books on the novel. Their writers are, on the whole, as disinclined as was H. G. Wells to look upon it as a means of relaxation. One point they are pretty unanimous on is that the story is of little consequence. Indeed, they are inclined to regard it as a hindrance to the reader's capacity to occupy himself with what in their opinion are the novel's significant elements. It does not seem to have occurred to them that the story, the plot, is as it were a lifeline which the author throws to the reader in order to hold his interest. They consider the telling of a story for its own sake as a debased form of fiction. That seems strange to me, since the desire to listen to stories appears to be as deeply rooted in the human animal as the sense of property. From the beginning of history men have gathered round the camp-fire, or in a group in the market place, to listen to the telling of a story. That the desire is as strong as ever is shown by the amazing popularity of detective stories in our own day. The fact remains that to describe a novelist as a mere storyteller is to dismiss him with contumely. I venture to suggest that there is no such creature. By the incidents he chooses to relate, the characters he selects and his attitude towards them, the author offers you a criticism of life. It may not be a very original one, or very profound, but it is there; and consequently, though he may not know it, he is in his own modest way a moralist. But morals, unlike mathematics, are not a precise science. Morals cannot be inflexible for they deal with the behaviour of human beings, and human beings, as we know, are vain, changeable and vacillating.

We live in a troubled world, and it is doubtless the novelist's business to deal with it. The future is uncertain. Our freedom is menaced. We are in the grip of anxieties, fears and frustrations. Values that were long unquestioned now seem dubious. But these are serious matters, and it has not escaped the writers of fiction that the reader may find a novel that is concerned with them somewhat heavy going. Now, owing to the invention of contraceptives, the high value that was once placed on chastity no longer obtains. Novelists have not been slow to notice the difference this has made in the relations of the sexes and so, whenever they feel that something must be done to sustain the reader's flagging interest, they cause their characters to indulge in copulation. I am not sure they are well-advised. Of sexual intercourse Lord Chesterfield said that the pleasure was momentary, the position ridiculous and the expense damnable: if he had lived to read modern fiction he might have added that there is a monotony about the act which renders the reiterated narration of it excessively tedious.

At present there is a tendency to dwell on characterization rather than on incident and, of course, characterization is important; for unless you come to know intimately the persons of a novel, and so can sympathize with them, you are unlikely to care what happens to them. But to concentrate on your characters, rather than on what happens to them, is merely one way of writing a novel like another. The tale of pure incident, in which the characterization is perfunctory or commonplace, has just as much right to exist as the other. Indeed, some very good novels of this kind have been written, *Gil Blas*, for instance, and *Monte Cristo*. Scheherazade would have lost her head very soon if she had dwelt on the characters of the persons she was dealing with, rather than on the adventures that befell them.

I have given in each case some account of the life and character of the author I am writing about. This I have done partly to please myself, but also for the reader's sake, since I think that to know what sort of a person the author is adds to one's understanding and appreciation of his work. To know something about Flaubert explains a good deal that would otherwise be disturbing in *Madame Bovary*, and to know the little there is to know about Emily Brontë gives a greater poignancy to her strange and wonderful book. A novelist myself, I have written these essays from my own standpoint. The danger of this is that the novelist is very apt to like best the sort of thing he himself does, and he will judge the work of others by how nearly they approach his own practice. In order to do full justice to works with which he has no natural sympathy, he needs a dispassionate integrity, a liberality of spirit, of which the members of an irritable race are seldom possessed. On the other hand, the critic who is not himself a creator is likely to know little about the technique of the novel, and so in his criticism he gives you either his personal impressions, which may well be of no great value, unless like Desmond MacCarthy he is not only a man of letters, but also a man of the world; or else he proffers a judgment founded on hard and fast rules which must be followed to gain his approbation. It is as though a shoemaker made shoes only in two sizes and if neither of them fitted your foot, you could for all he cared go shoeless.

The essays which are contained in this volume were written in the first place to induce readers to read the novels with which they are concerned, but in order not to spoil their pleasure it seemed to me that I had to take care not to reveal more of the story than I could help. That made it difficult to discuss the book adequately. In re-writing these pieces I have taken it for granted that the reader already knows the novels I treat of, and so it cannot matter to him if I divulge facts which the author has for obvious reasons delayed to the end to tell him. I have not hesitated to point out the defects as well as the merits that I see in these various novels, for nothing is of greater disservice to the general reader than the indiscriminate praise that is sometimes bestowed on certain works that are rightly accepted as classics. He reads and finds that such and such a motive is unconvincing, a certain character unreal, such and such an episode irrelevant and a certain description tedious. If he is of an impatient temper, he will cry that the critics who tell him that the novel he is reading is a masterpiece are a set of fools, and if he is of a modest one, he will blame himself and think that it is above his head and not for the likes of him; if, on the other hand, he is by nature dogged and persistent he will read on conscientiously, though without enjoyment. But a novel is to be read *with* enjoyment. If it doesn't give the reader that, it is, so far as he is concerned, valueless. In this respect every reader is his own best critic, for he alone knows what he enjoys and what he doesn't. I think, however, that the novelist may claim that you do not do him justice unless you admit that he has the right to demand something of his readers. He has the right to demand that they should possess the small amount of application that is needed to read a book of three or four hundred pages. He has the right to demand that they should have sufficient imagination to be able to interest themselves in the lives, joys and sorrows, tribulations, dangers and adventures of the characters of his invention. Unless a reader is able to give something of himself, he cannot get from a novel the best it has to give. And if he isn't able to do that, he had better not read it at all. There is no obligation to read a work of fiction.

Maugham's Selection of the Ten Best Novels

Henry Fielding and TOM JONES
Jane Austen and PRIDE AND PREJUDICE
Stendhal and LE ROUGE ET LE NOIR
Balzac and LE PERE GORIOT
Charles Dickens and DAVID COPPERFIELD
Flaubert and MADAME BOVARY
Herman Melville and MOBY DICK
Emily Brontë and WUTHERING HEIGHTS
Dostoevsky and THE BROTHERS KARAMAZOV
Tolstoy and WAR AND PEACE

From:

A Writer's Notebook

"Preface"

(1949)

The *Journal* of Jules Renard is one of the minor masterpieces of French literature. He wrote three or four one-act plays, which were neither very good nor very bad; they neither amuse you much nor move you much, but when well acted they can be sat through without ennui. He wrote several novels, of which one, *Poil de Carotte,* was very successful. It is the story of his own childhood, the story of a little uncouth boy whose harsh and unnatural mother leads him a wretched life. Renard's method of writing, without ornament, without emphasis, heightens the pathos of the dreadful tale, and the poor lad's sufferings, mitigated by no pale ray of hope, are heartrending. You laugh wryly at his clumsy efforts to ingratiate himself with that demon of a woman and you feel his humiliations, you resent his unmerited punishments, as though they were your own. It would be an ill-conditioned person who did not feel his blood boil at the infliction of such malignant cruelty. It is not a book that you can easily forget.

Jules Renard's other novels are of no great consequence. They are either fragments of autobiography or are compiled from the careful notes he took of people with whom he was thrown into close contact, and can hardly be counted as novels at all. He was so devoid of the creative power that one wonders why he ever became a writer. He had no invention to heighten the point of an incident or even to give a pattern to his acute observations. He collected facts; but a novel cannot be made of facts alone; in themselves they are dead things. Their use is to develop an idea or illustrate a theme, and the novelist not only has the right to change them to suit his purpose, to stress them or leave them in shadow, but is under the necessity of doing so. It is true that Jules Renard had his theories; he asserted that his object was merely to state, leaving the reader to write his own novel, as it were, on the data presented to him, and that to attempt to do anything else was literary fudge. But I am always suspicious of a novelist's theories; I have never known them to be anything other than a justification of his own shortcomings. So a writer who has no gift for the contrivance of a plausible story will tell you that story-telling is the least important part of the novelist's equipment, and if he is devoid of humour he will moan that humour is the death of fiction. In order to give the glow of life to brute fact it must be transmuted by passion, and so the only good novel Jules Renard wrote was when the passion of self-pity and the hatred he felt for his mother charged his recollections of his unhappy childhood with venom.

I surmise that he would be already forgotten but for the publication after his death of the diary that he kept assiduously for twenty years. It is a remarkable work. He knew a number of persons who were important in the literary and theatrical world of his day, actors like Sarah Bernhardt and Lucien Guitry, authors like Rostand and Capus, and he relates his various encounters with an admirable but caustic vivacity. Here his keen powers of observation were of service to him. But though his portraits have verisimilitude, and the lively conversation of these clever people has an authentic ring, you must have, perhaps, some knowledge of the world of Paris in the last few years of the nineteenth century and the first few years of the twentieth, either personal knowledge or knowledge by hearsay, really to ap-

preciate these parts of the journal. His fellow writers were indignant when the work was issued and they discovered with
what acrimony he had written of them. The picture he paints
of the literary life of his day is savage. They say dog does not
bite dog. That is not true of men of letters in France. In
England, I think, men of letters bother but little with one
another. They do not live in one another's pockets as French
authors do; they meet, indeed, infrequently, and then as
likely as not by chance. I remember one author saying to me
years ago: "I prefer to live with my raw material." They do
not even read one another very much. On one occasion, an
American critic came to England to interview a number of
distinguished writers on the state of English literature, and
gave up his project when he discovered that a very eminent
novelist, the first one he saw, had never read a single book
of Kipling's. English writers judge their fellow craftsmen;
one they will tell you is pretty good, another they will say
is no great shakes, but their enthusiasm for the former seldom
reaches fever-heat, and their disesteem for the latter is man-
ifested rather by indifference than by detraction. They do
not particularly envy someone else's success, and when it
is obviously unmerited, it moves them to laughter rather
than to wrath. I think English authors are self-centred. They
are, perhaps, as vain as any others, but their vanity is satisfied by the appreciation of a private circle. They are not
inordinately affected by adverse criticism, and with one or
two exceptions do not go out of their way to ingratiate
themselves with the reviewers. They live and let live.

Things are very different in France. There the literary life
is a merciless conflict in which one gives violent battle to
another, in which one clique attacks another clique, in which
you must be always on your guard against the gins and snares
of your enemies, and in which, indeed, you can never be
quite sure that a friend will not knife you in the back. It is
all against all, and, as in some forms of wrestling, anything
is allowed. It is a life of bitterness, envy and treachery, of

malice and hatred. I think there are reasons for this. One, of course, is that the French take literature much more seriously than we do, a book matters to them as it never matters to us, and they are prepared to wrangle over general principles with a vehemence that leaves us amazed—and tickled, for we cannot get it out of our heads that there is something comic in taking art so seriously. Then, political and religious matters have a way of getting themselves entangled with literature in France, and an author will see his book furiously assailed, not because it is a bad book, but because he is a Protestant, a nationalist, a communist or what not. Much of this is praiseworthy. It is well that a writer should think not only that the book he himself is writing is important, but that the books other people are writing are important too. It is well that authors, at least, should think that books really mean something, and that their influence is salutary, in which case they must be defended, or harmful, in which case they must be attacked. Books can't matter much if their authors themselves don't think they matter. It is because in France they think they matter so much that they take sides so fiercely.

There is one practice common to French authors that has always caused me astonishment, and that is their practice of reading their works to one another, either when they are in process of writing them, or when they have finished them. In England writers sometimes send their unpublished works to fellow craftsmen for criticism, by which they mean praise, for rash is the author who makes any serious objections to another's manuscript; he will only offend, and his criticism will not be listened to; but I cannot believe that any English author would submit himself to the excruciating boredom of sitting for hours while a fellow novelist reads him his latest work. In France it seems to be an understood thing that he should, and what is stranger, even eminent writers will often rewrite much of their work on the strength of the criticism they may have thus received. No less a person than

Flaubert acknowledges that he did so as a result of Turgenev's remarks, and you can gather from André Gide's
Journal that he has often profited in the same way. It has
puzzled me; and the explanation that I have offered to myself is that the French, because writing is an honourable
profession (which it has never been in England), often adopt
it without having any marked creative power; their keen
intelligence, their sound education and their background of
an agelong culture enable them to produce work of a high
standard, but it is the result of resolution, industry and a
well-stored, clever brain rather than of an urge to create, and
so criticism, the opinions of well-intentioned persons, can be
of considerable use. But I should be surprised to learn that
the great producers, of whom Balzac is the most eminent
example, put themselves to this trouble. They wrote because
they had to, and having written, thought only of what they
were going to write next. The practice proves, of course, that
French authors are prepared to take an immense deal of
trouble to make their works as perfect as may be, and that,
sensitive as they are, they have less self-complacency than
many of their English fellow craftsmen.

There is another reason why the antagonisms of authors in
France are more envenomed than in England; their public
is too small to support their great number: we have a public
of two hundred millions; they have one of forty. There is
plenty of room for every English writer; you may never have
heard of him, but if he has any gift at all, in any direction,
he can earn an adequate income. He is not very rich, but
then he would never have adopted the profession of letters
if riches had been his object. He acquires in time his body
of faithful readers, and since in order to get the publishers'
advertisements the papers are obliged to give a good deal of
space to reviews, he is accorded a sufficient amount of attention in the public Press. He can afford to look upon other
writers without envy. But in France few writers can make
a living by writing novels; unless they have private means or

some other occupation that enables them to provide for their needs, they are forced to resort to journalism. There are not enough book-buyers to go round, and the success of one author can greatly attenuate the success of another. It is a struggle to get known; it is a struggle to hold one's place in the public esteem. This results in frantic efforts to attract the benevolent attention of critics, and it is to the effect their reviews may have that must be ascribed the anxiety felt even by authors of reputation when they know that a notice is to appear in such and such a paper, and their fury when it is not a good one. It is true that criticism carries greater weight in France than it does in England. Certain critics are so influential that they can make or mar a book. Though every person of culture in the world reads French, and French books are read not only in Paris, it is only the opinion of Paris, of its writers, its critics, its intelligent public, that the French author really cares about. It is because literary ambition is centred in that one place that it is the scene of so much strife and heart-burning. And it is because the financial rewards of authorship are so small that there is so much eagerness, so much scheming to win the prizes that are every year awarded to certain books, or to enter into one or other of the academies which not only set an honourable seal on a career but increase an author's market value. But there are few prizes for the aspiring writer, few vacancies in the academies for the established one. Not many people know how much bitterness, how much bargaining, how much intrigue goes to the awarding of a prize or the election of a candidate.

But, of course, there are authors in France who are indifferent to money and scornful of honours, and since the French are a generous people, these authors are rewarded with the unqualified respect of all. That is why, indeed, certain writers who, judged by any reasonable standards, are evidently of no great consequence enjoy, especially among the young, a reputation that is incomprehensible to the foreigner. For unfortunately talent and originality do not always attend nobility of character.

Jules Renard was very honest, and he does not draw a pretty picture of himself in his *Journal*. He was malignant, cold, selfish, narrow, envious and ungrateful. His only redeeming feature was his love for his wife; she is the only person in all these volumes of whom he consistently speaks with kindness. He was immensely susceptible to any fancied affront, and his vanity was outrageous. He had neither charity nor good will. He splashes with his angry contempt everything he doesn't understand, and the possibility never occurs to him that if he doesn't the fault may lie in himself. He was odious, incapable of a generous gesture, and almost incapable of a generous emotion. But for all that the *Journal* is wonderfully good reading. It is extremely amusing. It is witty and subtle and often wise. It is a notebook kept for the purposes of his calling by a professional writer who passionately sought truth, purity of style and perfection of language. As a writer no one could have been more conscientious. Jules Renard jotted down neat retorts and clever phrases, epigrams, things seen, the sayings of people and the look of them, descriptions of scenery, effects of sunshine and shadow, everything, in short, that could be of use to him when he sat down to write for publication; and in several cases, as we know, when he had collected sufficient data he strung them together into a more or less connected narrative and made a book of them. To a writer this is the most interesting part of these volumes; you are taken into an author's workshop and shown what materials he thought worth gathering, and how he gathered them. It is not to the point that he lacked the capacity to make better use of them.

I forget who it was who said that every author should keep a notebook, but should take care never to refer to it. If you understand this properly, I think there is truth in it. By making a note of something that strikes you, you separate it from the incessant stream of impressions that crowd across the mental eye, and perhaps fix it in your memory. All of us have had good ideas or vivid sensations that we thought would one day come in useful, but which, because we were too lazy to write them down, have entirely escaped us. When you know you are going to make a note of something, you look at it more attentively than you otherwise would, and in the process of doing so the words are borne in upon you that will give it its private place in reality. The danger of using notes is that you find yourself inclined to rely on them, and so lose the even and natural flow of your writing which is somewhat pompously known as inspiration. You are also inclined to drag in your jottings whether they fit in or not. I have heard that Walter Pater used to make abundant notes on his reading and reflections and put them into appropriate pigeonholes, and when he had enough on a certain subject, fit them together and write an essay. If this is true, it may account for the rather cramped feeling one has when one reads him. This may be why his style has neither swing nor vigour. For my part, I think to keep copious notes is an excellent practice, and I can only regret that a natural indolence has prevented me from exercising it more diligently. They cannot fail to be of service if they are used with intelligence and discretion.

It is because Jules Renard's *Journal* in this respect so pleasantly engaged my attention that I have ventured to collect my own notes and offer them to the perusal of my fellow writers. I hasten to state that mine are not nearly so interesting as his. They are much more interrupted. There were many years in which I never kept notes at all. They do not pretend to be a journal; I never wrote anything about my meetings with interesting or famous people. I am sorry that I didn't. It would doubtless have made the following pages more amusing if I had recorded my conversations with the many and distinguished writers, painters, actors and politicians I have known more or less intimately. It never occurred to me to do so. I never made a note of anything that I did not think would be useful to me at one time or another in my work, and though, especially in the early notebooks, I jotted down all kinds of thoughts and emotions of a personal nature, it was only with the intention of ascribing them sooner or later to the creatures of my invention. I meant my notebooks to be a storehouse of materials for future use and nothing else.

As I grew older and more aware of my intentions, I used my notebooks less to record my private opinions, and more to put down while still fresh my impressions of such persons and places as seemed likely to be of service to me for the particular purpose I had in view at the moment. Indeed, on one occasion, when I went to China, vaguely thinking that I might write a book upon my travels, my notes were so copious that I abandoned the project and published them as they were. These, of course, I have omitted from this volume. I have likewise omitted everything I have elsewhere made use of, and if I have left in a phrase or two here and there that a diligent reader of my works recalls, it is not because I am so pleased with it that I want to repeat it, but from inadvertence. On one or two occasions, however, I have deliberately left in the facts that I noted down at the time and that gave me the idea for a story or a novel, thinking it might entertain the reader who chanced to remember one or the other, to see on what materials I devised a more elaborate piece. I have never claimed to create anything out of nothing; I have always needed an incident or a character as a starting point, but I have exercised imagination, invention and a sense of the dramatic to make it something of my own.

My early notebooks were largely filled with pages of dialogue for plays that I never wrote, and these, because I thought they could interest no one, I have also left out, but I have not left out a considerable number of remarks and reflections that seem to me now exaggerated and foolish. They are the expression of a very young man's reaction to real life, or what he thought was such, and to liberty, after the sheltered and confined existence, perverted by fond fancies and the reading of novels, which was natural to a boy in the class in which I was born; and they are the expression of his revolt from the ideas and conventions of the environment in which he had been brought up. I think I should have been dishonest with the reader if I had suppressed them. My first notebook is dated 1892; I was then eighteen. I have no wish to make myself out more sensible than I was. I was ignorant, ingenuous, enthusiastic and callow.

My notebooks amounted to fifteen stoutish volumes, but by omitting so much, as I have above described, I have reduced them to one no longer than many a novel. I hope the reader will accept this as a sufficient excuse for its publication. I do not publish it because I am so arrogant as to suppose that my every word deserves to be perpetuated. I publish it because I am interested in the technique of literary production and in the process of creation, and if such a volume as this by some other author came into my hands I should turn to it with avidity. By some happy chance what interests me seems to interest a great many other people; I could never have expected it, and I have never ceased to be surprised at it; but it may be that what has happened so often before will happen again, and some persons may be found who will discover here and there in the following pages something to interest them. I should have looked upon it as an impertinence to publish such a book when I was in the full flow of my literary activity; it would have seemed to claim an importance for myself which would have been offensive to my fellow writers; but now I am an old man, I can be no one's rival, for I have retired from the hurly-burly and ensconced myself not uncomfortably on the shelf. Any ambition I may have had has long since been satisfied. I contend with none, not because none is worth my strife, but because I have said my say and I am well pleased to let others occupy my small place in the world of letters. I have done what I wanted to do and now silence becomes me. I am told that in these days you are quickly forgotten if you do not by some new work keep your name before the public, and I have little doubt that it is true. Well, I am prepared for that. When my obituary notice at last appears in *The Times,* and they say: "What, I thought he died years ago," my ghost will gently chuckle.

"Foreword"

(1915)

This is a very long novel and I am ashamed to make it longer
by writing a preface to it. An author is probably the last
person who can write fitly about his own work. In this connection an instructive story is told by Roger Martin du Gard,
a distinguished French novelist, about Marcel Proust. Proust
wanted a certain French periodical to publish an important
article on his great novel and thinking that no one could
write it better than he, sat down and wrote it himself. Then
he asked a young friend of his, a man of letters, to put his
name to it and take it to the editor. This the young man did,
but after a few days the editor sent for him. "I must refuse
your article," he told him. "Marcel Proust would never forgive me if I printed a criticism of his work that was so perfunctory and so unsympathetic." Though authors are touchy
about their productions and inclined to resent unfavourable
criticism they are seldom self-satisfied. They are miserably
conscious how far the work on which they have spent much
time and trouble comes short of their conception and when
they consider it they are much more vexed with their failure
to express this in its completeness than pleased with the passages here and there that they can regard with complacency.
Their aim is perfection and they are wretchedly aware that
they have not attained it.

I will say nothing then about my book itself, but will content myself with telling the reader of these lines how a novel that has now had a fairly long life, as novels go, came to be written; and if it does not interest him I ask him to forgive me. I wrote it first when, at the age of twenty-three, having taken my medical degrees after five years at St. Thomas's Hospital, I went to Seville determined to earn my living as a writer. The manuscript of the book I wrote then still exists, but I have not looked at it since I corrected the typescript and I have no doubt that it is very immature. I sent it to Fisher Unwin, who had published my first book (while still a medical student I had published a novel called *Liza of Lambeth*, which had had something of a success), but he refused to give me the hundred pounds I wanted for it and none of the other publishers to whom I afterwards submitted it would have it at any price. This distressed me at the time, but now I know that I was very fortunate; for if one of them had taken my book (it was called *The Artistic Temperament of Stephen Carey*) I should have lost a subject which I was too young to make proper use of. I was not far enough away from the events I described to use them properly and I had not had a number of experiences which later went to enrich the book I finally wrote. Nor had I learnt that it is easier to write of what you know than of what you don't. For instance, I sent my hero to Rouen (which I knew only as an occasional visitor) to learn French, instead of to Heidelberg (where I had been myself) to learn German.

Thus rebuffed I put the manuscript away. I wrote other novels, which were published, and I wrote plays. I became a very successful playwright and determined to devote the rest of my life to the drama. But I reckoned without a force within me that made my resolutions vain. I was happy, I was prosperous, I was busy. My head was full of the plays I wanted to write. I do not know whether it was that success did not bring me all I had expected or whether it was a natural reaction from it, but I was but just firmly established as the most popular dramatist of the day when I began once more to be obsessed by the teeming memories of my past life. They came back to me so pressingly, in my sleep, on my walks, at rehearsals, at parties, they became such a burden to me, that I made up my mind there was only one way to be free of them and that was to write them all down in a book. After submitting myself for some years to the exigencies of the drama I hankered after the wide liberty of the novel. I knew the book I had in mind would be a long one and I wanted to be undisturbed, so I refused the contracts that managers were eagerly offering me and temporarily retired from the stage. I was then thirty-seven.

For long after I became a writer by profession I spent much time on learning how to write and subjected myself to very tiresome training in the endeavour to improve my style. But these efforts I abandoned when my plays began to be produced and when I started to write again it was with different aims. I no longer sought a jewelled prose and a rich texture, on unavailing attempts to achieve which I had formerly wasted much labour; I sought on the contrary plainness and simplicity. With so much that I wanted to say within reasonable limits I felt that I could not afford to waste words and I set out now with the notion of using only such as were necessary to make my meaning clear. I had no space for ornament. My experience in the theatre had taught me the value of succinctness and the danger of beating about the bush. I worked unremittingly for two years. I did not know what to call my book and after looking about a great deal hit upon *Beauty from Ashes*, a quotation from Isaiah which seemed to me apposite; but learning that this title had been recently used was obliged to search for another. I chose finally the name of one of the books in Spinoza's *Ethics* and called it *Of Human Bondage*. I have a notion I was once more lucky in finding that I could not use the first title I had thought of.

Of Human Bondage is not an autobiography, but an autobiographical novel; fact and fiction are inextricably mingled;

the emotions are my own, but not all the incidents are related as they happened and some of them are transferred to
my hero not from my own life but from that of persons with
whom I was intimate. The book did for me what I wanted
and when it was issued to the world (a world in the throes of
a dreadful war and too much concerned with its own sufferings and fears to bother with the adventures of a creature of
fiction) I found myself free forever from the pains and unhappy recollections that had tormented me. It was very well
reviewed; Theodore Dreiser wrote for *The New Republic* a
long criticism in which he dealt with it with the intelligence
and sympathy which distinguish everything he has ever
written; but it looked very much as though it would go the
way of the vast majority of novels and be forgotten for ever a
few months after its appearance. But, I do not know through
what accident it happened after some years that it attracted
the attention of a number of distinguished writers in the
United States and the references they continued to make to
it in the press gradually brought it to the notice of the public. To these writers is due the new lease of life that the book
was thus given and them must I thank for the success it has
continued increasingly to have as the years go by.

I hope the reader will not accuse me of stupid egotism if
I hazard the suggestion that the form of drama that I knew is
destined to end very soon, and of course I do not mean for
any such foolish reason as that I ceased to write. Realistic
drama in prose is a form of art, though a minor one, and a
minor art, responding to a particular state in civilisation, is
likely to perish with a change in that state. The history of
prose drama is short. It seems to have sprung into life here
and there, during the sixteenth century, in rude farces like
those played by Tabarin in a booth to attract customers for
his quack medicines. In Spain it quickly achieved uncommon
merit in the racy plays of Lope de Rueda, but was killed by
the greater attractiveness to the public of verse. It was raised
to a form of art by Molière, flourished with his reflected light
in the comedies of the Restoration, and was practised with
elegance by Marivaux and Beaumarchais in the France of
the eighteenth century; it throve with increasing luxuriance
in France during the next hundred years, and was cultivated
by a long series of men of talent. It reached its utmost height
in the solid work of Ibsen. It seems to me that Ibsen brought
the realistic prose drama to such perfection as it is capable

of, and in the process killed it. His plays seem stagy enough now; *When We Dead Awaken*, which many good judges think an important work, is a piece of theatrical clap-trap that you cannot believe in for a moment; but it was his influence that finally stripped the drama of those elements of recreation which, in my opinion, are essential to it. The dramatists have wilfully cast aside the ornaments that made their plays an entertainment for the eye and ear. The desire for verisimilitude has resulted in an intolerable dullness. Realism, where realism is out of place, has forced the dramatists in order to hold the attention of their audience to resort to themes outside the normal run of life, and so is responsible for the plays of murder and detection that give, with all their absurdities, the opportunity for thrilling incident.

The great dramatists of the past sacrificed truth of characterisation and probability of incident to situation, which (to my mind, rightly) they considered the essence of drama. But the interest of the present day is in the analysis of character. I think this is something new, and points to a change of civilisation, and this, as I suggested just now, entails the death of a form of art that was sustained by it. The characters of the older fiction were static; Balzac and Dickens told you all about their persons when they first brought them before your notice, and they remained unaltered, whatever happened to them and however long a period elapsed, till their authors had finished with them. This view of human nature evidently suited the prepossessions of the time, and it was perfectly convenient to the playwright. It enabled him to make his characters consistent and distinct. But the characters of fiction now are diverse and unstable. It has been found that the novelist can get all the excitement of a tale of adventure by the gradual disclosure of a person's character; in other cases he is concerned to show the changes in it that are occasioned by lapse of time and the circumstances of life. He examines, sometimes naively, sometimes subtly, the contradictions of human nature, and his readers are ready to take an interest in the complexity of the man in the street. All this is very difficult for the dramatist to deal with, and he has discarded the two devices, the soliloquy and the aside, by which he might have achieved at least some success. The burden is thrown upon the actors to translate into flesh and blood the conventional hieroglyphs which are all the dramatist can provide them with. It is too great a burden. The spectator no longer believes in the persons that are set before him.

But my melancholic prognosis applies only to the modern realistic prose drama. I do not mean of course that the drama can die. Its long history shows that like music, painting, architecture and poetry it responds to a permanent need of the human race. But when a form of art has reached what perfection it is capable of and then decays there is nothing to do but return to its origins. You have an example in sculpture at the present day which is finding a new inspiration in the wood-carving of the negroes and in the stone work of the Mayan and Peruvian craftsmen. The early drama amused the eye with spectacle and dancing and the ear with verse and music. I think the modern playwright would do well to call in these allied arts to his help. I do not suppose blank verse can profitably be used again, but a quick, running metre like that used by the old Spanish dramatists, though with less frequent rhymes, may well be acceptable, not only to the 'chosen few', but to the public at large. A long tirade in verse, as everyone knows who has seen a play of Racine, has apart from the sense, by its volume of rhythmical sound, a very high dramatic value. I do not see why music should not be used, as in the old melodramas, to prepare a mood or emphasise an emotion. There is no need to remark on the diverting effect of beautiful scenes and gay costumes or on the agreeableness of good dancing. An ingenious dramatist should be able to make all these an integral part of his play. With such pleasant means of recreation he may render attractive that drama of the soul which, as I have suggested, seems the natural development forced upon him by the success of the cinema.

But I would not condemn the dramatist to occupy himself only with high and serious matters. Comedy also has its claims. It has been greatly hampered by the demand for verisimilitude. My good fortune has brought me in contact with most of the celebrated wits of my day; and I have noticed that they sparkle but intermittently; no one in private life shines so continuously as a witty character should in a play, he is never so pointed, finished and apt; the conversation of a comedy is artificial in its essence, and to take pains to make it resemble the conversation of real life is absurd. The aim of comedy is not to represent life, but amusingly to comment on it. There is no valid reason why farce should not enter into it. In practice it is almost impossible to hold the attention of an audience for two hours and a half with pure comedy. But when the humours grow broad the critics shake their heads and, mildly or acrimoniously, regret the introduction of horse-play. I think they make a mistake. Comedy, depending as it does on wit, appeals only to the intellect; that is not enough: farce appeals to the belly. The great comic writers of the past felt no fear of it, and I would have the comic writers of the future feel no fear of it either, but use it, as freely as Aristophanes and Molière, whenever it suits their purpose. They must not mind if the very superior look down their noses. They can always console themselves with the recollection that Walter Pater laughed consumedly at *The Magistrate*.

From:

The Complete Short Stories of
W. Somerset Maugham

Volume I—East and West

This book contains thirty stories. They are all about the same length and on the same scale. The first was written in 1919 and the last in 1931. Though in early youth I had written a number of short stories, for a long time, twelve or fifteen years at least, occupied with the drama, I had ceased to do so; and when a journey to the South Seas unexpectedly provided me with themes that seemed to suit this medium, it was as a beginner of over forty that I wrote the story which is now called *Rain*. Since it caused some little stir the reader of this preface will perhaps have patience with me if I transcribe the working notes, made at the time, on which it was constructed. They are written in hackneyed and slipshod phrases, without grace; for nature has not endowed me with the happy gift of hitting instinctively upon the perfect word to indicate an object and the unusual but apt adjective to describe it. I was travelling from Honolulu to Pago Pago and, hoping they might at some time be of service, I jotted down as usual my impressions of such of my fellow-passengers as attracted my attention. This is what I said of Miss Thompson: "Plump, pretty in a coarse fashion, perhaps not more than twenty-seven. She wore a white dress and a large white hat, long white boots from which the calves bulged in cotton stockings." There had been a raid on the Red Light district in Honolulu just before we sailed and the gossip of the ship spread the report that she was making the journey to escape arrest. My notes go on: "W. *The Missionary*. He was a tall thin man, with long limbs loosely jointed, he had hollow cheeks and high cheek bones, his fine, large, dark eyes were deep in their sockets, he had full sensual lips, he wore his hair rather long. He had a cadaverous air and a look of suppressed fire. His hands were large, with long fingers, rather finely shaped. His naturally pale skin was deeply burned by the tropical sun. *Mrs. W. His Wife.* She was a little woman with her hair very elaborately done, New England; not prominent blue eyes behind gold-rimmed pince-nez, her face was long like a sheep's, but she gave no impression of foolishness, rather of extreme alertness. She had the quick movements of a bird. The most noticeable thing about her was her voice, high, metallic, and without inflection; it fell on the ear with a hard monotony, irritating to the nerves like the ceaseless clamour of a pneumatic drill. She was dressed in black and wore round her neck a gold chain from which hung a small cross." She told me that W. was a missionary on the Gilberts and his district consisting of widely separated islands he frequently had to go distances by canoe. During this time she remained at headquarters and managed the mission. Often the seas were very rough and the journeys were not without peril. He was a medical missionary. She spoke of the depravity of the natives in a voice which nothing could hush, but with a vehement, unctuous horror, telling me of their marriage customs which were obscene beyond description. She said, when first they went it was impossible to find a single good girl in any of the villages. She inveighed against dancing. I talked with the missionary and his wife but once, and with Miss Thompson not at all. Here is the note for the story: "A prostitute, flying from Honolulu after a raid, lands at Pago Pago. There lands there also a missionary and his wife. Also the narrator. All are obliged to stay there owing to an outbreak of measles. The missionary finding out her profession persecutes her. He reduces her to misery, shame, and repentance, he has no mercy on her. He induces the governor to order her return to Honolulu. One morning he is found with his throat cut by his own hand and she is once more radiant and self-possessed. She looks at men and scornfully exclaims: 'dirty pigs.'"

An intelligent critic, who combines wide reading and a sensitive taste with a knowledge of the world rare among those who follow his calling, has found in my stories the influence of Guy de Maupassant. That is not strange. When I was a boy he was considered the best short story writer in France and I read his works with avidity. From the age of fifteen whenever I went to Paris I spent most of my afternoons poring over the books in the galleries of the Odéon. I have never passed more enchanted hours. The attendants in their long smocks were indifferent to the people who sauntered about looking at the books and they would let you read for hours without bothering. There was a shelf filled with the works of Guy de Maupassant, but they cost three francs fifty a volume and that was not a sum I was prepared to spend. I had to read as best I could standing up and peering between the uncut pages. Sometimes when no attendant was looking I would hastily cut a page and thus read more conveniently. Fortunately some of them were issued in a cheap edition at seventy-five centimes and I seldom came away without one of these. In this manner, before I was eighteen, I had read all the best stories. It is natural enough that when at that age I began writing stories myself I should unconsciously have chosen those little masterpieces as a model. I might very well have hit upon a worse.

Maupassant's reputation does not stand as high as it did, and it is evident now that there is much in his work to repel. He was a Frenchman of his period in violent reaction against the romantic age which was finishing in the saccharine sentimentality of Octave Feuillet (admired by Matthew Arnold) and in the impetuous slop of George Sand. He was a naturalist, aiming at truth at all costs, but the truth he achieved looks to us now a trifle superficial. He does not analyse his characters. He takes little interest in the reason why. They act, but wherefore he does not know. "For me," he says, "psychology in a novel or in a story consists in this: to show the inner man by his life." That is very well, that is what we all try to do, but the gesture will not by itself always indicate the motive. The result with Maupassant was a simplification of character which is effective enough in a short story, but on reflection leaves you unconvinced. There is more in men than that, you say. Again, he was obsessed by the tiresome notion, common then to his countrymen, that it was a duty a man owed himself to hop into bed with every woman under forty that he met. His characters indulge their sexual desire to gratify their self-esteem. They are like the people who eat caviar when they are not hungry because it is expensive. Perhaps the only human emotion that affects his characters with passion is avarice. This he can understand; it fills him with horror, but notwithstanding he has a sneaking sympathy with it. He was slightly common. But for all this it would be foolish to deny his excellence. An author has the right to be judged by his best work. No author is perfect. You must accept his defects; they are often the necessary complement of his merits; and this may be said in gratitude to posterity that it is very willing to do this. It takes what is good in a writer and is not troubled by what is bad. It goes so far sometimes, to the confusion of the candid reader, as to claim a profound significance for obvious faults. So you will see the critics (the awe-inspiring voice of posterity) find subtle reasons to explain to his credit something in a play of Shakespeare's that any dramatist could tell them needed no other explanation than haste, indifference or wilfulness. Maupassant's stories are good stories. The anecdote is interesting apart from the narration so that it would secure attention if it were told over the dinner-table; and that seems to me a very great merit indeed. However halting your words and insipid your rendering, you could not fail to interest your listeners if you told them the bare story of *Boule de Suif*, *L'Héritage* or *La Parure*. These stories have a beginning, a middle and an end. They do not wander along an uncertain line so that you cannot see whither they are leading, but follow without hesitation, from exposition to climax, a bold and vigorous curve. It may be that they have no great spiritual significance. Maupassant did not aim at that. He looked upon himself as a plain man; no good writer was ever less a man of letters. He did not pretend to be a philosopher, and here he was well-advised, for when he indulges in reflection he is commonplace. But within his limits he is admirable. He has an astonishing capacity for creating living people. He can afford little space, but in a few pages can set before you half a dozen persons so sharply seen and vividly described that you know all about them that you need. Their outline is clear; they are distinguishable from one another; and they breathe the breath of life. They have no complexity, they lack strangely the indecision, the unexpectedness, the mystery that we see in human beings; they are in fact simplified for the purposes of the story. But they are not deliberately simplified: those keen eyes of his saw clearly, but they did not see profoundly; it is a happy chance that they saw all that was necessary for him to achieve the aim he had in view. He treats the surroundings in the same way, he sets his scene accurately, briefly and effectively; but whether he is describing the charming landscape of Normandy or the stuffy, overcrowded drawing-rooms of the eighties his object is the same, to get on with the story. On his own lines I do not think that Maupassant is likely to be surpassed. If his excellence is not at the moment so apparent it is because what he wrote must now stand comparison with the very different, more subtle and moving work of Chekhov.

His stories are the models that young writers naturally take. This is understandable. On the face of it it is easier to write stories like Chekhov's than stories like Maupassant's. To invent a story interesting in itself apart from the telling is a difficult thing, the power to do it is a gift of nature, it cannot be acquired by taking thought, and it is a gift that very few people have. Chekhov had many gifts, but not this one. If you try to tell one of his stories you will find that there is nothing to tell. The anecdote, stripped of its trimmings, is insignificant and often inane. It was grand for people who wanted to write a story and couldn't think of a plot to discover that you could very well manage without one. If you could take two or three persons, describe their mutual relations and leave it at that, why then it wasn't so hard to write a story; and if you could flatter yourself that this really was art, what could be more charming?

But I am not quite sure that it is wise to found a technique on a writer's defects. I have little doubt that Chekhov would have written stories with an ingenious, original and striking plot if he had been able to think of them. It was not in his temperament. Like all good writers he made a merit of his limitations. Was it not Goethe who said that an artist only achieves greatness when he recognises them? If a short story is a piece of prose dealing with more or less imaginary persons no one wrote better short stories than Chekhov. If, however, as some think, it should be the representation of an action, complete in itself and of a certain limited length, he leaves something to be desired. He put his own idea clearly enough in these words: "Why write about a man getting into a submarine and going to the North Pole to reconcile himself to the world, while his beloved at that moment throws herself with a hysterical shriek from the belfry? All this is untrue and does not happen in real life. One must write about simple things: how Peter Semionovitch married Maria Ivanovna. That is all." But there is no reason why a writer should not make a story of an unusual incident. The fact that something happens every day does not make it more important. The pleasure of recognition, which is the pleasure thus aimed at, is the lowest of the aesthetic pleasures. It is not a merit in a story that it is undramatic. Maupassant chose very ordinary people and sought to show what there was of drama in the common happenings of their lives. He chose the significant incident and extracted from it all the drama possible. It is a method as praiseworthy as another; it tends to make a story more absorbing. Probability is not the only test; and probability is a constantly changing thing. At one time it was accepted that the "call of the blood" should enable long-lost children to recognize their parents and that a woman only had to get into men's clothes to pass as a man. Probability is what you can get the readers of your time to swallow. Nor did Chekhov, notwithstanding his principles, adhere to his canon unless it suited him. Take one of the most beautiful and touching of his stories, *The Bishop*. It describes the approach of death with great tenderness, but there is no reason for the Bishop to die, and a better technician would have made the cause of death an integral part of the story. "Everything that has no relation to the story must be ruthlessly thrown away," he says in his advice to Schoukin. "If in the first chapter you say that a gun hung on the wall, in the second or third chapter it must without fail be discharged." So when the Bishop eats some tainted fish and a few days later dies of typhoid we may suppose that it was the tainted fish that killed him. If that is so he did not die of typhoid, but of ptomaine poisoning, and the symptoms were not as described. But of course Chekhov did not care. He was determined that his good and gentle bishop should die and for his own purposes he wanted him to die in a particular way. I do not understand the people who say of Chekhov's stories that they are slices of life, I do not understand, that is, if they mean that they offer a true and typical picture of life. I do not believe they do that, nor do I believe they ever did. I think they are marvellously lifelike, owing to the writer's peculiar talent, but I think they are deliberately chosen to square with the prepossessions of a sick, sad and overworked, gray-minded man. I do not blame them for that. Every writer sees the world in his own way and gives you his own picture of it. The imitation of life is not a reasonable aim of art; it is a discipline to which the artist from time to time subjects himself when the stylization of life has reached an extravagance that outrages common sense. For Chekhov

life is like a game of billiards in which you never pot the red,
bring off a losing hazard or make a cannon, and should you
by a miraculous chance get a fluke you will almost certainly
cut the cloth. He sighs sadly because the futile do not suc-
ceed, the idle do not work, liars do not speak the truth,
drunkards are not sober and the ignorant have no culture. I
suppose that it is this attitude that makes his chief characters
somewhat indistinct. He can give you a striking portrait of a
man in two lines, as much as can be said of anyone in two
lines to set before you a living person, but with elaboration
he seems to lose his grasp of the individual. His men are
shadowy creatures, with vague impulses to good, but without will-power, shiftless, untruthful, fond of fine words, often
with great ideals, but with no power of action. His women
are lachrymose, slatternly and feeble-minded. Though they
think it a sin they will commit fornication with anyone who
asks them, not because they have passion, not even because
they want to, but because it is too much trouble to refuse. It
is only in his description of young girls that he seems touched
with a tender indulgence. "Alas! regardless of their doom,
the little victims play." He is moved by their charm, the
gaiety of their laughter, their ingenuousness and their vitality; but it all leads to nothing. They make no effort to con-
quer their happiness, but yield passively to the first obstacle
in the way.

But if I have ventured to make these observations I beg
the reader not to think that I have anything but a very great
admiration for Chekhov. No writer, I repeat, is faultless. It is
well to admire him for his merits. Not to recognize his
imperfections, but rather to insist that they are excellencies,
can in the long run only hurt his reputation. Chekhov is extremely readable. That is a writer's supreme virtue and one
upon which sufficient stress is often not laid. He shared it
with Maupassant. Both of them were professional writers
who turned out stories at more or less regular intervals to
earn their living. They wrote as a doctor visits his patients

or a solicitor sees his clients. It was part of the day's work. They had to please their readers. They were not always inspired, it was only now and then that they produced a masterpiece, but it is very seldom that they wrote anything that did not hold the reader's attention to the last line. They both wrote for papers and magazines. Sometimes a critic will describe a book of short stories as magazine stories and thus in his own mind damn them. That is foolish. No form of art is produced unless there is a demand for it and if newspapers and magazines did not publish short stories they would not be written. All stories are magazine stories or newspaper stories. The writers must accept certain (but constantly changing) conditions; it has never been shown yet that a good writer was unable to write his best owing to the conditions under which alone he could gain a public for his work. That has never been anything but an excuse of the second-rate. I suspect that Chekhov's great merit of concision is due to the fact that the newspapers for which he habitually wrote could only give him a certain amount of space. He said that stories should have neither a beginning nor an end. He could not have meant that literally. You might as well ask of a fish that it should have neither head nor tail. It would not be a fish if it hadn't. The way Chekhov in reality begins a story is wonderfully good. He gives the facts at once, in a few lines; he has an unerring feeling for the essential statements, and he sets them down baldly, but with great precision, so that you know at once whom you have to deal with and what the circumstances are. Maupassant often started his stories with an introduction designed to put the reader in a certain frame of mind. It is a dangerous method only justified by success. It may be dull. It may throw the reader off the scent; you have won his interest in certain characters and then instead of being told what you would like to know about them, your interest is claimed for other people in other circumstances. Chekhov preached compactness. In his longer stories he did not always achieve it. He was distressed by the charge brought against him that he was indifferent to moral and sociological questions and when he had ample space at his command he seized the opportunity to show that they meant as much to him as to any other right-thinking person. Then in long and somewhat tedious conversations he would make his characters express his own conviction that, whatever the conditions of things might be then, at some not far distant date (say 1934) the Russians would be free, tyranny would exist no longer, the poor would hunger no more and happiness, peace and brotherly love rule in the vast empire. But these were aberrations forced upon him by the pressure of opinion (common in all countries) that the writer of fiction should be a prophet, a social reformer and a philosopher. In his shorter stories Chekhov attained the concision he aimed at in a manner that is almost miraculous.

And no one had a greater gift than he for giving you the intimate feeling of a place, a landscape, a conversation or (within his limited range) a character. I suppose this is what people mean by the vague word atmosphere. Chekhov seems to have achieved it very simply, without elaborate explanation or long description, by a precise narration of facts; and I think it was due with him to a power of seeing things with amazing naïvety. The Russians are a semi-barbarous people and they seem to have retained the power of seeing things naturally, as though they existed in a vacuum; while we in the West, with our complicated culture behind us, see things with the associations they have gathered during long centuries of civilization. They almost seem to see the thing in itself. Most writers, especially those living abroad, have in the last few years been shown numbers of stories by Russian refugees who vainly hope to earn a few guineas by placing them somewhere. Though dealing with the present day they might very well be stories by Chekhov not at his best; they all have that direct, sincere vision. It is a national gift. In no one was it more acutely developed than in Chekhov.

But I have not yet pointed out what to my mind is Chekhov's greatest merit. Since I am not a critic and do not know the proper critical expressions I am obliged to describe this as best I can in terms of my own feeling. Chekhov had an amazing power of surrounding people with air so that, though he does not put them before you in the round and they lack the coarse, often brutal vitality of Maupassant's figures, they live with a strange and unearthly life. They are not lit by the hard light of common day but suffused in a mysterious grayness. They move in this as though they were disembodied spirits. It is their souls that you seem to see. The subconscious seems to come to the surface and they communicate with one another directly without the impediment of speech. Strange, futile creatures, with descriptions of their outward seeming tacked on them like a card on an exhibit in a museum, they move as mysteriously as the tortured souls who crowded about Dante when he walked in Hell. You have the feeling of a vast, gray, lost throng wandering aimless in some dim underworld. It fills you with awe and with uneasiness. I have hinted that Chekhov had no great talent for inventing a multiplicity of persons. Under different names, with different environment, the same characters recur. It is as though, when you looked at the soul, the superficial difference vanishes and everyone is more or less the same. His people seem strangely to slip into one another as though they were not distinct individuals, but temporary fictions, and as though in truth they were all part of one another. The importance of a writer in the long run rests on his uniqueness. I do not know that anyone but Chekhov has so poignantly been able to represent spirit communing with spirit. It is this that makes one feel that Maupassant in comparison is obvious and vulgar. The strange, the terrible thing is that, looking at man in their different ways, these two great writers, Maupassant and Chekhov, saw eye to eye. One was content to look upon the flesh, the other, more nobly and subtly, surveyed the spirit; but they agreed that life was

tedious and insignificant and that men were base, unintel-
ligent and pitiful.

I hope the reader will not be impatient with me because
in an introduction to my own stories I have dwelt at length
on these remarkable writers. Maupassant and Chekhov are
the two authors of short stories whose influence survives to
the present day and all of us who cultivate the medium must
in the end be judged by the standards they have set.

So far as I could remember it I have placed the stories in
this volume in the order in which they were written. I
thought it might possibly interest the reader to see how I
had progressed from the tentativeness of the first ones, when
I was very much at the mercy of my anecdote, to the relative
certainty of the later ones when I had learnt so to arrange my
material as to attain the result I wanted. Though all but two
have been published in a magazine these stories were not
written with that end in view. When I began to write them
I was fortunately in a position of decent independence and
I wrote them as a relief from work which I thought I had
been too long concerned with. It is often said that stories are
no better than they are because the editors of magazines insist on their being written to a certain pattern. This has not
been my experience. All but *Rain* and *The Book-Bag* were
published in the *Cosmopolitan* magazine and Ray Long, the
Editor, never put pressure on me to write other than as I
wished. Sometimes the stories were cut and this is reasonable
since no editor can afford one contributor more than a certain
amount of space; but I was never asked to make the smallest
alteration to suit what might be supposed to be the taste of
the readers. Ray Long paid me for them not only with good
money, but with generous appreciation. I did not value this
less. We authors are simple, childish creatures and we treas-
ure a word of praise from those who buy our wares. Most of
them were written in groups from notes made as they occurred to me, and in each group I left naturally enough to
the last those that seemed most difficult to write. A story is

difficult to write when you do not know *all* about it from the beginning, but for part of it must trust to your imagination and experience. Sometimes the curve does not intuitively present itself and you have to resort to this method and that to get the appropriate line.

I beg the reader not to be deceived by the fact that a good many of these stories are told in the first person into thinking that they are experiences of my own. This is merely a device to gain verisimilitude. It is one that has its defects, for it may strike the reader that the narrator could not know all the events he sets forth; and when he tells a story in the first person at one remove, when he reports, I mean, a story that someone tells him, it may very well seem that the speaker, a police officer, for example, or a sea-captain, could never have expressed himself with such facility and with such elaboration. Every convention has its disadvantages. These must be as far as possible disguised and what cannot be disguised must be accepted. The advantage of this one is its directness. It makes it possible for the writer to tell no more than he knows. Making no claim to omniscience, he can frankly say when a motive or an occurrence is unknown to him, and thus often give his story a plausibility that it might otherwise lack. It tends also to put the reader on intimate terms with the author. Since Maupassant and Chekhov, who tried so hard to be objective, nevertheless are so nakedly personal, it has sometimes seemed to me that if the author can in no way keep himself out of his work it might be better if he put in as much of himself as possible. The danger is that he may put in too much and thus be as boring as a talker who insists on monopolizing the conversation. Like all conventions this one must be used with discretion. The reader may have observed that in the original note of *Rain* the narrator was introduced, but in the story as written omitted.

Three of the stories in this volume were told me and I had nothing to do but make them probable, coherent and dramatic. They are *The Letter*, *Footprints in the Jungle* and

The Book-Bag. The rest were invented, as I have shown
Rain was, by the accident of my happening upon persons
here and there, who in themselves or from something I heard
about them suggested a theme that seemed suitable for a
short story. This brings me to a topic that has always concerned writers and that has at times given the public, the
writer's raw material, some uneasiness. There are authors
who state that they never have a living model in mind when
they create a character. I think they are mistaken. They are
of this opinion because they have not scrutinized with sufficient care the recollections and impressions upon which
they have constructed the person who, they fondly imagine,
is of their invention. If they did they would discover that,
unless he was taken from some book they had read, a practice by no means uncommon, he was suggested by one or
more persons they had at one time known or seen. The great
writers of the past made no secret of the fact that their characters were founded on living people. We know that the good
Sir Walter Scott, a man of the highest principles, portrayed
his father, with sharpness first and then, when the passage
of years had changed his temper, with tolerance; Henri
Beyle, in the manuscript of at least one of his novels, has
written in at the side the names of the real persons who were
his models; and this is what Turgenev himself says: "For my
part, I ought to confess that I never attempted to create a
type without having, not an idea, but a living person, in
whom the various elements were harmonized together, to
work from. I have always needed some groundwork on which
I could tread firmly." With Flaubert it is the same story; that
Dickens used his friends and relations freely is notorious;
and if you read the *Journal* of Jules Renard, a most instructive book to anyone who wishes to know how a writer works,
you will see the care with which he set down every little
detail about the habits, ways of speech and appearance of
the persons he knew. When he came to write a novel he
made use of this storehouse of carefully collected infor-

mation. In Chekhov's diary you will find notes which were obviously made for use at some future time, and in the recollections of his friends there are frequent references to the persons who were the originals of certain of his characters. It looks as though the practice were very common. I should have said it was necessary and inevitable. Its convenience is obvious. You are much more likely to depict a character who is a recognizable human being, with his own individuality, if you have a living model. The imagination can create nothing out of the void. It needs the stimulus of sensation. The writer whose creative faculty has been moved by something peculiar in a person (peculiar perhaps only to the writer) falsifies his idea if he attempts to describe that person other than as he sees him. Character hangs together and if you try to throw people off the scent, by making a short man tall for example (as though stature had no effect on character) or by making him choleric when he has the concomitant traits of an equable temper, you will destroy the plausible harmony (to use the beautiful phrase of Baltasar Gracian) of which it consists. The whole affair would be plain sailing if it were not for the feelings of the persons concerned. The writer has to consider the vanity of the human race and the Schadenfreude which is one of its commonest and most detestable failings. A man's friends will find pleasure in recognizing him in a book and though the author may never even have seen him will point out to him, especially if it is unflattering, what they consider his living image. Often someone will recognize a trait he knows in himself or a description of the place he lives in and in his conceit jumps to the conclusion that the character described is a portrait of himself. Thus in the story called *The Outstation* the Resident was suggested by a British Consul I had once known in Spain and it was written ten years after his death, but I have heard that the Resident of a district in Sarawak, which I described in the story, was much affronted because he thought I had had him in mind. The two men had not a trait in common. I do not suppose any writer attempts to draw an exact portrait. Nothing, indeed, is so unwise as to put into a work of fiction a person drawn line by line from life. His values are all wrong, and, strangely enough, he does not make the other characters in the story seem false, but himself. He never convinces. That is why the many writers who have been attracted by the singular and powerful figure of the late Lord Northcliffe have never succeeded in presenting a credible personage. The model a writer chooses is seen through his own temperament and if he is a writer of any originality what he sees need have little relation with the facts. He may see a tall man short or a generous one avaricious; but, I repeat, if he sees him tall, tall he must remain. He takes only what he wants of the living man. He uses him as a peg on which to hang his own fancies. To achieve his end (the plausible harmony that nature so seldom provides) he gives him traits that the model does not possess. He makes him coherent and substantial. The created character, the result of imagination founded on fact, is art, and life in the raw, as we know, is of this only the material. The odd thing is that when the charge is made that an author has copied this person or the other from life, emphasis is laid only on his less praiseworthy characteristics. If you say of a character that he is kind to his mother, but beats his wife, everyone will cry: Ah, that's Brown, how beastly to say he beats his wife; and no one thinks for a moment of Jones and Robinson who are notoriously kind to their mothers. I draw from this the somewhat surprising conclusion that we know our friends by their vices and not by their virtues. I have stated that I never even spoke to Miss Thompson in *Rain*. This is a character that the world has not found wanting in vividness. Though but one of a multitude of writers my practice is doubtless common to most, so that I may be permitted to give another instance of it. I was once asked to meet at dinner two persons, a husband and wife, of whom I was told only what the reader will shortly read. I think I never knew their names. I should certainly not recognize them if I met them in the street. Here are the notes I made at the time. "A stout, rather pompous man of fifty, with pince-nez, gray-haired, a florid complexion, blue eyes, a neat gray moustache. He talks with assurance. He is resident of an outlying district and is somewhat impressed with the importance of his position. He despises the men who have let themselves go under the influence of the climate and the surroundings. He has travelled extensively during his short leaves in the East and knows Java, the Philippines, the coast of China and the Malay Peninsula. He is very British, very patriotic; he takes a great deal of exercise. He has been a very heavy drinker and always took a bottle of whisky to bed with him. His wife has entirely cured him and now he drinks nothing but water. She is a little insignificant woman, with sharp features, thin, with a sallow skin and a flat chest. She is very badly dressed. She has all the prejudices of an Englishwoman. All her family for generations have been in second-rate regiments. Except that you know that she has caused her husband to cease drinking entirely you would think her quite colourless and unimportant." On these materials I invented the story which is called *Before the Party*. I do not believe that any candid person could think that these two people had cause for complaint because they had been made use of. It is true that I should never have thought of the story if I had not met them, but anyone who takes the trouble to read it will see how insignificant was the incident (the taking of the bottle to bed) that suggested it and how differently the two chief characters have in the course of writing developed from the brief sketch which was their foundation.

"Critics are like horse-flies which prevent the horse from ploughing," said Chekhov. "For over twenty years I have read criticisms of my stories, and I do not remember a single remark of any value or one word of valuable advice. Only once Skabichevsky wrote something which made an impression on me. He said I would die in a ditch, drunk." He was writing for twenty-five years and during that time his writing was constantly attacked. I do not know whether the critics of the present day are naturally of a less ferocious temper; I must allow that on the whole the judgment that has been passed on the stories in this volume when from time to time a collection has been published in book form has been favourable. One epithet, however, has been much applied to them, which has puzzled me; they have been described with disconcerting frequency as "competent." Now on the face of it I might have thought this laudatory, for to do a thing competently is certainly more deserving of praise than to do it incompetently, but the adjective has been used in a disparaging sense and, anxious to learn and if possible to improve, I have asked myself what was in the mind of the critics who thus employed it. Of course none of us is liked by everybody and it is necessary that a man's writing, which is so intimate a revelation of himself, should be repulsive to persons who are naturally antagonistic to the creature he is. This should leave him unperturbed. But when an author's work is somewhat commonly found to have a quality that is unattractive to many it is sensible of him to give the matter his attention. There is evidently something that a number of people do not like in my stories and it is this they try to express when they damn them with the faint praise of competence. I have a notion that it is the definiteness of their form. I hazard the suggestion (perhaps unduly flattering to myself) because this particular criticism has never been made in France where my stories have had with the critics and the public much greater success than they have had in England. The French, with their classical sense and their orderly minds, demand a precise form and are exasperated by a work in which the ends are left lying about, themes are propounded and not resolved and a climax is foreseen and then eluded. This precision on the other hand has always been slightly antipathetic to the English. Our great novels have been shapeless and this, far from disconcerting their readers, has given them a sense of security. This is the life we know, they have thought, with its arbitrariness and inconsequence; we can put out of our minds the irritating thought that two and two make four. If I am right in this surmise I can do nothing about it and I must resign myself to being called competent for the rest of my days. My prepossessions in the arts are on the side of law and order. I like a story that fits. I did not take to writing stories seriously till I had had much experience as a dramatist, and this experience taught me to leave out everything that did not serve the dramatic value of my story. It taught me to make incident follow incident in such a manner as to lead up to the climax I had in mind. I am not unaware of the disadvantages of this method. It gives a tightness of effect that is sometimes disconcerting. You feel that life does not dovetail into its various parts with such neatness. In life stories straggle, they begin nowhere and tail off without a point. That is probably what Chekhov meant when he said that stories should have neither a beginning nor an end. It is certain that sometimes it gives you a sensation of airlessness when you see persons who behave so exactly according to character, and incidents that fall into place with such perfect convenience. The story-teller of this kind aims not only at giving his own feelings about life, but at a formal decoration. He arranges life to suit his purposes. He follows a design in his mind, leaving out this and changing that; he distorts facts to his advantage, according to his plan; and when he attains his object produces a work of art. It may be that life slips through his fingers; then he has failed; it may be that he seems sometimes so artificial that you cannot believe him, and when you do not believe a story-teller he is done. When he succeeds he has forced you for a time to accept his view of the universe and has given you the pleasure of following out the pattern he has drawn on the surface of chaos. But he seeks to prove nothing. He paints a picture and sets it before you. You can take it or leave it.

From:

The Complete Short Stories of
W. Somerset Maugham

Volume II — The World Over

This book contains all the stories I have written that are not included in *East and West*. The tales in that collection were of about the same length and written on the same scale and so it seemed convenient to publish them together in a single volume. Most of the stories which I have now gathered together are very much shorter. Some were written many years ago, others more recently. They appeared in magazines and were afterwards issued in book form. To the first lot I gave the title of *Cosmopolitans*, because they were offered to the public in the *Cosmopolitan* magazine, and except for Ray Long, who was then its editor, would never have been written.

When I was in China in 1920 I took notes of whatever I saw that excited my interest, with the intention of making a connected narrative out of them; but when I came home and read them it seemed to me that they had a vividness which I might easily lose if I tried to elaborate them. So I changed my mind and decided to publish them as they stood under the title: *On a Chinese Screen*. Ray Long chanced to read this and it occurred to him that some of my notes might well be taken for short stories. I have included two of them, "The Taipan" and "The Consul," in this volume. The fact is that if you are a storyteller any curious person you meet has a way of suggesting a story, and incidents that to others will seem quite haphazard have a way of presenting themselves to you with the pattern your natural instinct has impressed on them.

Magazine readers do not like starting a story and, after reading for a while, being told to turn to page one hundred and something. Writers do not like it either, for they think the interruption disturbs the reader and they have besides an uneasy fear that sometimes he will not take the trouble and so leave their story unfinished. There is no help for it. Everyone should know that a magazine costs more to produce than it is sold for, and could not exist but for the advertisements. The advertisers think that their announcements are more likely to be read if they are on the same page as matter which they modestly, but often mistakenly, think of greater interest. So in the illustrated periodicals it has been found advisable to put the beginning of a story or an article, with the picture that purports to illustrate it, at the beginning and the continuation with the advertisements later on.

Neither readers nor writers should complain. Readers get something for far less than cost price and writers are paid sums for their productions which only the advertisements render possible. They should remember that they are only there as bait. Their office is to fill blank spaces and indirectly induce their readers to buy motor accessories, aids to beauty and join correspondence courses. Fortunately this need not affect them. The best story from the advertisers' standpoint (and they make their views felt on this question) is the story that gives readers most entertainment. Ray Long conceived the notion that the readers of the *Cosmopolitan* would like it if they were given at least one story that they could read without having to hunt for the continuation among the advertisements, and he commissioned me to write half a dozen sketches of the same sort as those in *On a Chinese Screen*. They were to be short enough to print on opposite pages of the magazine and leave plenty of room for illustration.

The sketches I wrote pleased and the commission was renewed. I went on writing them until my natural verbosity got the better of me and I found myself no longer able to keep my stories within the limits imposed upon me. Then I had to stop. I think I learned a good deal from the writing of them and I am glad that I did. My difficulty was to compress what I had to tell into a number of words which must not be exceeded and yet leave the reader with the impression that I had told all there was to tell. It was this that made the enterprise amusing. It was also salutary. I could not afford to waste a word. I had to be succinct. I was surprised to find how many adverbs and adjectives I could leave out without any harm to the matter or the manner. One often writes needless words because they give the phrase balance. It was very good practice to try to get it into a sentence without using a word that was not necessary to the sense.

The matter, of course, had to be chosen with discretion; it would have been futile to take a theme that demanded elaborate development. I have a natural predilection for completeness, so that even in the little space at my disposal I wanted my story to have a certain structure. I do not care for the shapeless story. To my mind it is not enough when the writer gives you the plain facts seen through his own eyes (which means of course that they are not plain facts, but facts coloured by his own idiosyncrasy); I think he should impose a pattern on them. Naturally these stories are anecdotes. If stories are interesting and well told they are none the worse for that. The anecdote is the basis of fiction. The restlessness of writers forces upon fiction from time to time forms that are foreign to it, but when it has been oppressed for a period by obscurity, propaganda or affectation, it reverts, and returns inevitably to the proper function of fiction, which is to tell an interesting story.

In the preface to *East and West* I said pretty well all I had to say about the short story in general. I have nothing to add to that. I have written now nearly a hundred stories and one thing I have discovered is that whether you hit upon a story or not, whether it comes off or not, is very much a matter of luck. Stories are lying about at every street corner, but the writer may not be there at the moment they are waiting to be picked up or he may be looking at a shop window and pass them unnoticed. He may write them before he has seen all there is to see in them or he may turn them over in his mind so long that they have lost their freshness. He may not have seen them from the exact standpoint at which they can be written to their best advantage. It is a rare and happy event when he conceives the idea of a story, writes it at the precise moment when it is ripe, and treats it in such a way as to get out of it all that it implicitly contains. Then it will be within its limitations perfect. But perfection is seldom achieved. I think a volume of modest dimensions would contain all the short stories which even closely approach it. The reader should be satisfied if in any collection of these short pieces of fiction he finds a general level of competence and on closing the book feels that he has been amused, interested and moved.

With one exception all the stories I have written have been published in magazines. The exception is a story called "The Book-Bag." When I sent it to Ray Long he wrote to me, in sorrow rather than in anger, that he had gone further with me than with any other author, but when it came to incest he had to draw the line. I could not blame him. He published the tale later in a collection of what he thought in his long career as editor of the *Cosmopolitan* were the best short stories that had ever been offered him. I know that in admitting that my stories have been published in magazines I lay myself open to critical depreciation, for to describe a tale as a magazine story is to condemn it. But when the critics do this they show less acumen than may reasonably be expected of them. Nor do they show much knowledge of literary history. For ever since magazines became a popular form of publication authors have found them a useful medium to put their work before readers. All the greatest short-story writers have published their stories in magazines, Balzac, Flaubert and Maupassant; Chekhov, Henry James, Rudyard Kipling. I do not think it rash to say that the only short stories that have not been published in a magazine are the stories that no editor would accept. So to damn a story because it is a magazine story is absurd. The magazines doubtless publish a great many bad stories, but then more bad stories are written than good ones, and an editor, even of a magazine with literary pretensions, is often obliged to print a story of which he doesn't think highly because he can get nothing better. Some editors of popular magazines think their readers demand a certain type of story and will take nothing else; and they manage to find writers who can turn out the sort of thing they want and often make a very good job of it. This is the machine-made article that has given the magazine story a bad name. But after all, no one is obliged to read it. It gives satisfaction to many people since it allows them for a brief period to experience in fancy the romance and adventure which in the monotony of their lives they crave for.

But if I may judge from the reviews I have read of the volumes of short stories that are frequently published, where the critics to my mind err is when they dismiss stories as magazine stories because they are well constructed, dramatic and have a surprise ending. There is nothing to be condemned in a surprise ending if it is the natural end of a story. On the contrary it is an excellence. It is only bad when, as in some of O. Henry's stories, it is dragged in without reason to give the reader a kick. Nor is a story any the worse for being neatly built, with a beginning, a middle and an end. All good story writers have done their best to achieve this. It is the fashion of today for writers, under the influence of an inadequate acquaintance with Chekhov, to write stories that begin anywhere and end inconclusively. They think it enough if they have described a mood, or given an impression, or drawn a character. That is all very well, but it is not a story, and I do not think it satisfies the reader. He does not like to be left wondering. He wants to have his questions answered. That is what I have tried to do, and when a story was suggested to me of which I didn't know the answer I forbore to write it. One such story I wrote about in *A Writer's*

Notebook, and since I don't expect everyone to have read everything I have written I think it may amuse the reader if I here repeat it. When I was in India I received a letter from a man unknown to me in which he told me the following incident in the belief that I might be able to make use of it:

Two young fellows were working on a tea plantation in the hills and the mail had to be fetched from a long way off so that they only got it at rather long intervals. One of the young fellows, let us call him A, got a lot of letters by every mail, ten or twelve and sometimes more, but the other, B, never got one. He used to watch A enviously as he took his bundle and started to read; he hankered to have a letter, just one letter; and one day, when they were expecting the mail, he said to A: "Look here, you always have a packet of letters ¡and I never get any. I'll give you five pounds if you'll let me have one of yours." "Right-ho," said A, and when the mail came in he handed B his letters and said to him: "Take whichever you like." B gave him a five-pound note, looked over the letters, chose one and returned the rest. In the evening when they were having whisky and soda before dinner, A asked casually: "By the way, what was that letter about?" "I'm not going to tell you," said B. A, somewhat taken aback, said: "Well, who was it from?" "That's my business," answered B. They had a bit of an argument, but B stood on his rights and refused to say anything about the letter he had bought. A began to fret, and as the weeks went by he did all he could to persuade B to let him see the letter. B continued to refuse. At length A, anxious, worried, and curious, felt he couldn't bear it any longer, so he went to B and said: "Look here, here's your five pounds, let me have my letter back again." "Not on your life," said B. "I bought it and paid for it, it's my letter and I'm not going to give it up."

In *A Writer's Notebook* I added: "I suppose if I belonged to the modern school of story writers I should write it just as it is and leave it. It goes against the grain with me. I want a story to have form, and I don't see how you can give it that unless you can bring it to a conclusion that leaves no legitimate room for questioning. But even if you could bring yourself to leave the reader up in the air you don't want to leave yourself up in the air with him." The facts as my correspondent gave them to me intrigued a good many people, and a magazine in Canada and *The New Statesman* in England, independently of one another, offered prizes to their readers for the best conclusion to the story. I don't know that the results were particularly successful.

I read once an article on how to write a short story. Certain points the author made were useful, but to my mind the central thesis was wrong. She stated that the "focal point" of a short story should be the building of character and that the incidents should be invented solely to "liven" personality. Oddly enough she remarked earlier in her article that the parables are the best short stories that have ever been written. I think it would be difficult to describe the characters of the Prodigal Son and his brother or of the Good Samaritan and the Man who fell among thieves. They are in fact not characterized and we have to guess what sort of people they were, for we are only told about them the essential facts necessary for the pointing of the moral. And that, whether he has a moral to point or not, is about all the short-story writer can do. He has no room to describe and develop a character; at best he can only give the salient traits that bring the character to life and so make the story he has to tell plausible. Since the beginning of history men have gathered around the campfire or in a group in the market place to listen to the telling of stories. The desire to listen to them appears to be as deeply rooted in the human animal as the sense of property. I have never pretended to be anything but a storyteller. It has amused me to tell stories and I have told a great many.

I have been writing stories for fifty years. In that long period I have seen a number of bright stars creep shyly over the horizon, travel across the sky to burn with a more or less gem-like flame for a while in mid-heaven, and then dwindle into an obscurity from which there is little likelihood that they will ever emerge. The writer has his special communication to make, which, when you come to analyse it, is the personality with which he is endowed by nature, and during the early years of his activity he is groping in the dark to express it; then, if he is fortunate, he succeeds in doing this and if there is in his personality a certain abundance he may contrive for a long time to produce work which is varied and characteristic; but the time comes at last (if he is so imprudent as to live to a ripe age) when, having given what he has to give, his powers fail. He has fashioned all the stories he himself is capable of digging out of the inexhaustible mine which is human nature and he has created all the characters which can possibly be constituted out of the various sides of his own personality. For no one, I believe, can create a character from pure observation; if it is to have life it must be at least in some degree a representation of himself. A generation has arisen which is strange to him and it is only by an effort of will that he can understand the interests of a world of which he can now be only an observer. But to understand is not enough; the writer of fiction must feel, and he must not only feel with, he must feel in. It is well then if he can bring himself to cease writing stories which might just as well have remained unwritten. He is wise to watch warily for the signs which will indicate to him that having said his say, it behoves him to resign himself to silence.

I have written my last story.

Part II

CONCERNING
THE WORKS OF OTHER WRITERS

For complete listing of these works, consult pages 153 to 158.

Traveller's Library

There are people who have no head for cards. It is impossible
not to be sorry for them, for what, one asks oneself, can the
future have to offer them when the glow of youth has de-
parted and advancing years force them, as they force all of
us, to be spectators rather than actors in the comedy of life?
Love is for the young and affection is but a frigid solace to
a pining heart. Sport demands physical vigour and affairs a
strenuous activity. To have learnt to play a good game of
bridge is the safest insurance against the tedium of old age.
Throughout life one may find in cards endless entertainment
and an occupation for idle hours that rests the mind from
care and pleasantly exercises the intelligence. For the people
who say that only the stupid can play cards err; they do not
know what decision, what quickness of apprehension, what
judgment, what knowledge of character, are required to play
a difficult hand perfectly. The good card-player trusts his intuition as implicitly as Monsieur Bergson, but he calls it a
hunch; the brilliant card-player has a gift as specific as the
poet's: he too is born not made. The student of human nature can find endless matter for observation in the behaviour
of his fellow card-players. Meanness and generosity, pru-
dence and audacity, courage and timidity, weakness and
strength; all these men show at the card-table according to
their natures, and because they are intent upon the game

drop the mask they wear in the ordinary affairs of life. Few are so deep that you do not know the essential facts about them after a few rubbers of bridge. The card-table is a very good school for the study of mankind. The unhappy persons who have no card sense say that playing cards is a waste of time, but it is never waste of time to amuse oneself; and besides, the day has twenty-four hours and the week seven days, there is always a certain time to be wasted. In passing I may remark that even *they* generally own a greasy pack of cards, and when you come upon them unexpectedly you are just as likely to find them occupied in laying out a patience as in improving their minds with great literature or their souls with reflection. Of course when you ask them how leisure can be better employed they say, in conversation. For they are great talkers. They lament the decay of the art of conversation and ascribe it to the universal passion for bridge. It is obvious that this pastime has deprived many a light prattler of his audience and it is true that there are now few conversationalists in the grand style. I doubt whether the impatience of the present day would suffer their tyranny, for they seem to have indulged much in monologue and they were impatient of interruption. I have a notion that it is pleasanter to read Boswell's record of the conversations than it ever was to listen to Dr. Johnson. I have heard that when Mallarmé received his admirers on those Tuesdays which literary gossip has made famous, he stood in front of the fireplace and discoursed on some subject or other amid the silence of the company; and certainly the accounts one hears of the conversation of Anatole France do not lead one to suspect that there was much give and take. I should have thought that sort of thing must have been an interesting experience, and maybe an intellectual treat, but hardly a pleasant relaxation. It can indeed only have been supportable because the listeners were filled with awe of the speaker, and awe, happily, is not a feeling that we, English and Americans, particularly cherish for men of eminence. On the other hand, ordinary conversation, the chit-chat of the drawing-room, is seldom in English-speaking countries witty or profound. Its staple is the foibles of our friends and the affairs of the day. We are shy of speaking in public of our souls, of God and Immortality, and we are rarely so interested in art and literature as to be willing to argue about them. The accompaniment of good music is needed to loosen our tongues. It is not often in a mixed gathering that conversation proceeds long without some of us hankering after the bridge-table, and if there is no sign of it glancing surreptitiously at our watches and wondering how soon we can decently take our leave. It is to meet this situation, I suppose, that in circles where cards are not played the games have been invented that add so much horror to social intercourse, such as Lights, Consequences and Anagrams. There are even people who have brought the torture of their fellows to such a pitch that they force you to invent rhymed couplets upon topics of their suggestion. Such diversions of course point to an abnormal pleasure in the infliction of boredom.

Perhaps the least intolerable of all these methods of passing time is to offer for discussion some point of behaviour. If, for instance, in some disaster you could only save one person and your choice lay between a small boy, a beautiful young woman and an eminent scientist, which would you choose? Another is, if you were going to spend the rest of your life on a desert island and could only take twelve books which would they be? This question occurred to me when I set about choosing the materials for the volume to which this is the introduction. It is of course no test of one's literary inclinations, for in such a case the amount of matter would have to be the first consideration. People very sensibly for the most part mention the Bible and the plays of Shakespeare. I have read the Bible twice through from cover to cover and have no great wish to read it again, but it certainly contains a lot of meat and I suppose would be a good book to take. The same may be said of Shakespeare. There are

many of the plays which no one would in ordinary circumstances care to read a second time, but none that if you were
pressed for reading matter you could not read at least once
or twice a year. After these two the choice becomes more
difficult and the answers vary; but the question of quantity
is as important as that of quality and the whole of Wordsworth in one volume would evidently be preferred to the
whole of Keats. And then you must consider that you will
have to read the same thing twenty, fifty or a hundred times.
There are a great many books that are worth reading once,
a considerable number that are worth reading twice, but not
many that are worth reading over and over again. I once
knew a man who read *The Pickwick Papers* every year for
thirty years, but he eventually died of cirrhosis of the liver.

In the collection of pieces that comprise this book I have
not sought to provide a volume for anyone who looks forward
to being cast away on a desert island. My object is modest.
I have asked myself what I should like to take with me in a
single volume of reasonable size if I could have but one book
and were travelling from New York to San Francisco by train
or across the Atlantic on a tramp steamer. I do not want to
tire the reader of this preface with a long account of the
reasons for which I have inserted this or that, but I should
like him to have patience with me while I tell him exactly
what I have been at. I am not a critic or a scholar. Either
of these would doubtless have chosen very different things
from what I have, but if the publishers of this volume had
needed the taste of the one or the learning of the other I
should certainly not have been invited to make the selection.
I am a professional writer. I have read a great deal, sometimes
for instruction and sometimes for pleasure, but never since
I was a small boy without an inward eye on the relation
between what I was reading and my professional interests.
At one time I read omnivorously, but for a good many years
I have read little but what immediately concerned me. I am
sure that a great deal that was worth reading has thus es-

caped me. For this reason the reader will doubtless look in vain for much that he would have expected to find here. I am more interested in an author's personality than in the books he writes. I follow him in the attempts he makes to express himself, his experiments in this manner and that; but when he has produced the work in which he has at last said all he has to say about himself, when he has arrived at what perhaps for many years he has only approached, then I read him no longer. At least if I do it is out of politeness, because he has given me his book, or fear, in case he should be affronted if I didn't, and not from inclination. Sometimes I have to read many books by an author before my curiosity about him is satisfied and sometimes only his first or second. He may write half a hundred masterpieces after that, but life is short and there is a great deal I urgently want to read, and I am content to leave their enjoyment to others. I dare say some of the authors represented in this volume are not represented by their best things. I dare say they have written since much of greater merit, but I do not happen to have read it. These writers belong roughly to the same period. It is difficult to appreciate any generation but one's own. Few of the writers who were esteemed of importance when I was a young man excite me much now and even then I was doubtless more critical than became me. The young author may be forgiven if he is unfair to his elders. They occupy a place in the sun which he would gladly fill. But it is not only envy that leads him to depreciate them. For they deal with manners and customs that have constrained his youth; they represent an attitude towards life and deliver a philosophy which he is naturally in revolt against. They are realists and he is a romantic or the other way about. He cannot be expected to realise that his attitude and his philosophy will in a little while seem as dull and conventional as those that now outrage his sense of common decency. And it is easy to miss the merits of the writers who are pushing one into the background. I have always a sneaking sympathy with George Crabbe who read the poems of Byron, Walter Scott, Keats and Shelley, and thought them all stuff and nonsense. After all he might have been right. In the case of one of them he was, and perhaps of two. I would offer it as a test that an author can apply to himself; when he can see nothing at all in work that the best critical opinion of the day pronounces good, his hour has struck and nothing remains to him but to shut up shop and like Voltaire's Candide cultivate a garden. It is dangerous for an author to get too set in his own manner and I have always followed, though with circumspection, the productions of my fellow writers in order to see whether in technique or point of view they could teach me something that it behoved me to know. But during the forty years I have been studying my craft I have seen so many writers hailed as masters, enjoy their hour of glory, and sink into an oblivion which is always described as well-merited, that I have become sceptical; and now, when a new genius is discovered I wait a year or two before I concern myself with him. It is astonishing how many books I find there is no need for me to read at all. This volume then does not pretend to be a survey of English literature during the last thirty years or so, but merely a hap-hazard collection of pieces that I have read and thought I should like to read again. I have chosen them from the work of English writers partly because I know current English literature better than current American literature and because it seemed to me that by keeping to the authors of one country I obtained at least an illusion of unity, which is the only completeness such a miscellany can hope to have; but also because American literature during the last thirty years is so rich, especially in the short story, a form I am particularly attracted by, and in the light novel, a form not often successfully cultivated in England, that I should have been overwhelmed by the mass of matter. I could never have got into the limits of this book half the things I should have urgently wanted to put in. I have in point of fact read again all that is here offered to the reader and I think that it is good. When I was gathering the materials I made a list of a number of things that I thought I should like to include, but when I came to tackle them found that many of them did not bear a second reading. I made some unforeseen discoveries. Stories that I had thought profound now seemed to me pretentious and others that I had thought humorous, silly; verses that had moved me left me cold and essays I had found suggestive I now found trivial. I have thrown many old friends into the dustbin; but not without a sigh. Lest the kindly reader should think me heartless I hasten to add that I speak metaphorically; I have in fact put them in a large packing-case and sent them to the local hospital.

The ablest editor I know is accustomed to say: I am the average American and what interests me will interest my readers; the event has proved him right. Now I have most of my life been miserably conscious that I am not the average Englishman. Let no one think I say this with self-satisfaction, for I think that there is nothing better than to be like everybody else. It is the only way to be happy, and it is with but a wry face that one tells oneself that happiness is not everything. The best writers have been ordinary men and it is because they felt all the emotions of ordinary men that (with genius to help) they have been able to represent human beings with truth and sympathy. It is impossible to draw a complete picture of men unless you can think with their heads and feel with their hearts. There have of course been many excellent writers who in one way or another were abnormal and they have produced works that have a tang and an originality that make them sometimes more readable than the work of the greater writers, but I do not think they can be said ever to have reached those wonderful heights on which the Olympians dwell. I find *Wuthering Heights* more interesting than *David Copperfield,* but I have no doubt which is the greater novel. The accident of my birth in France, which enabled me to learn French and English simultaneously and thus instilled into me two modes of life, two liberties, two points of view, has prevented me from ever identifying myself completely with the instincts and prejudices of one people or the other, and it is in instinct and prejudice that sympathy is most deeply rooted; the accident of a physical infirmity, with its attendant nervousness, separated me to a greater extent than would be thought likely from the common life of others. In my communications with my fellows I have generally felt 'out of it'; in that uprush of emotion that sometimes seizes a crowd so that their hearts throb as one I have been lamentably aware that my own keeps its accustomed and normal rhythm. When 'Everybody suddenly burst out singing' as Siegfried Sassoon says in one of the most moving of the poems I have been allowed to reprint in this book, I have always felt exceedingly embarrassed. And when on New Year's Eve people join hands and swinging them up and down to the music, like a nurse rocking the baby, sing lustily *Should Auld Acquaintance be Forgot*, my shivering nerves whisper, yes, please. I cannot then offer this book as the choice of the average man and I cannot say that because these things please me they will please you. If you like me they will please you, and if you don't they won't. Though I do not share many of the prejudices that many people have, I naturally have prejudices of my own, and they will be obvious to anyone who reads this book through. I am a writer and I look at these things from my professional standpoint. This is the difference between the writer and the critic, that the critic, the good one, can look upon productions from the vantage-ground of the absolute and putting himself in the author's shoes can judge of the success of his efforts without the hindrance of predisposition. I do not think that many writers can do this. However good a book may be we can difficultly find merit in it if it is not the sort of thing we do, or think we can do ourselves. Mr. E. M. Forster not very long ago wrote a book called *Aspects of the Novel*. In a novel of mine I ventured on a little gibe

at his expense, but Mr. Forster is a man of great disinterest-
edness, generous of soul, and with a delicate sense of humour; I think he forgave me my jest for he was good enough
to write and tell me that he liked my book. His, nevertheless, is a good one, interesting not only to the novelist but
also to the novel-reader; but I speak of it now to suggest that
an acute reader could certainly divine from it what sort of
novels Mr. Forster would write. He makes much of just those
characteristics in which no one now writing is richer than
himself, but holds cheap that element of the novel, the story,
in which, I venture to think, his own weakness lies. My private opinion is that if Mr. Forster, with his gift for beautiful
English, his power of creating significant, interesting and living persons, his emotion and humour, his poetic feeling,
could or would submit himself to the indignity of devising
a good story he would write a novel that would make his
eminent talent manifest to the whole world. But my opinion
is neither here nor there. In this volume there is nothing
that I would not have been glad to write myself. Of course
I know that there is a great deal that I have not the gift to
write. When I was young in moments of passion I used to
beat my fists on the writing table and cry, but God, I wish
I had more brains; but now, resigned though far from content, I am prepared to make do with what I have. Just as
there are painters' pictures, there are writers' books. There
are also readers' books. These are books that a reader enjoys but a writer, knowing the trick, finds intolerable. They
are written to a formula. The author has set himself too easy
a task. It is as if you expected a juggler to be amused by a
child bouncing a ball. But they are sometimes very well done.
They are often painstaking and sincere. When I start on a
novel in which there is an elderly man, generally in the lower
ranks of life, married to a young wife, and an adolescent, his
son or a farmhand in the offing, my heart sinks. The course
of the story, with its powerful scenes, is obvious to me. This
kind of book is much praised for its 'strength.' But there may

be as much 'strength' in a woman offering another a cup of tea as in a man kicking his wife to death with hob-nailed boots. The action is but a symbol. Dialect is the last straw. I do not like yokels who exchange wise cracks. Any workaday novelist knows that that sort of thing can be turned out by the yard and he laughs up his sleeve at the simplicity of the reading public that can find amusement in a form of humour so mechanical. Another kind that comes for me under the head of readers' books is the whimsical. These are much written by the literary sort of critics who think they will take a rest from serious work. They are often cultured and written with distinction. They have what is generally described as a charming fantasy. The formula here is simple. A middle-aged literary man takes a holiday in the country and on his walks meets a leprechaun and exchanges pleasantly philosophical remarks with him; or a young poet seeks lodgings in a London suburb where the maid-of-all-work is of an astonishing beauty; she converses with an ingenuousness that brings a lump to your throat, and there is certainly another lodger, a middle-aged literary man, who makes pleasantly philosophical remarks. Generally somebody dies in the end and it makes a very pathetic scene. There are very delicate descriptions of scenery. The reader will find nothing of the kind in these pages. He will find humour and he will find pathos. He will not find the namby-pamby.

Nor will he find the didactic. Of late years the novel as everyone knows has widened its scope; it has become a platform for the exposition of the author's ideas. Novelists have become politicians, economists, social reformers and what not. They have used the novel to advocate this cause and that. They have been deeply concerned with the vital problems of the day. For this, I think, we may hold the Russians responsible. The Russian novelists brought something new to fiction, but by the circumstances of their civilisation they were inclined to subordinate art to social questions. Chekhov, as we know, was much blamed for his indifference to them and his defenders were at pains to rebut the charge. They did not come out into the open and claim that he was an artist and that was enough, but sought chapter and verse to prove that his aim in describing the Russian peasant, for instance, was purely humanitarian. But the novelists who concern themselves with such things run a double danger. The first is that their views are unlikely to be sound (if they had the scientific instinct they would not be novelists) and the second is that the problems they deal with have seldom more than a temporary interest. What are you to say of a novel that becomes unreadable when an act of Parliament has changed a law? I forget what critic it was that said that the subject of great poetry was the common vicissitudes of humanity, birth and death, love and hatred, youth and old age. I venture to think that these are also the subjects of great fiction. I know it is out of fashion just now to think that the object of art is to entertain. I cannot help it. When I want instruction I go to philosophers, men of science and historians; I do not ask the novelist to give me anything but amusement. I am not in bad company, for Corneille (after Aristotle) thought that the pleasure of his audience was the poet's only aim, and the tender and perfect Racine contended, even with acrimony, that the first rule of the drama was to please and all the others were devised merely to achieve that end. And did not the philosophic Coleridge say that the object of poetry was delight? The unfortunate remark made by Terence in a play that few have read has had a disastrous effect on novelists. Of course it is very well that their sympathies should be universal, but that does not prove that their opinions are valuable. My uncle, a clergyman, told one of his curates who had a discordant voice and insisted on singing in church that it would be to the greater glory of God if he praised him only in his heart. I wonder if the writers of fiction who are so determined to teach us and improve us noticed that the other day a racing motorist who had driven a car faster than anyone else in the world was

brought up on to a public platform to tell the free-born elec-
tors of a great constituency how they should vote on a question concerning the relations between the British Empire and
India. There is a certain vulgarity in setting yourself up as an
authority in matters on which your knowledge can be but
superficial. I do not see why the story-teller should not be
content to be a story-teller. He can be an artist and is that
so little?

I read in the papers that rhetoric is coming into fashion
again; and an eminent anthologist (but a less eminent novelist) is, I hear, bringing out a collection entirely devoted to
purple passages. I shall not read it. In poetry, which is the
happy avocation of youth, I do not mind, in moderation, a
little rhetoric, but I do not like it in prose at all. I think the
reader will find little in the following pages that is not written
with simplicity. In my youth, influenced by the fashion of
the day, I did my best to write in the grand manner. I studied
the Bible, I sought phrases in the venerable Hooker and copied out passages of Jeremy Taylor. I ransacked the dictionary
for unusual epithets. I went to the British Museum and made
lists of the names of precious stones. But I had no bent that
way and, resigning myself to writing not as I should have
liked but as I could, I returned to the study of Swift. In passing I should like to suggest that the Bible has not had an
altogether happy influence on English style. No one would
deny that it is a great monument of the language, but after
all it is a translation and its grandiloquent imagery is alien
to our natures. For long I thought that Swift was the best
model on which the modern English writer could form his
style, and I still think there is something intoxicating in the
order in which he places his words. But now I find in him a
certain dryness and a dead level which is somewhat tiring.
He is like a man who, whatever his emotion and however
emphatic his words, never raises his voice. It is a little sinis-
ter. I think if I were starting over again I should devote myself to the study of Dryden. It was he who first gave English

prose its form. He released the language from the ponderous eloquence that had overwhelmed it and made it the lovely supple instrument which at its best it is. He had the straight-forwardness and the limpidity of Swift; but a melodious variety and a conversational ease that Swift never attained. He had a happy charm of which the Dean was incapable. Swift's English flows like the water in a canal shaded by neat poplars, but Dryden's like a great river under the open sky. I know none more delightful. Of course a living language changes and it would be absurd for anyone to try to write like Dryden now. But his excellencies are still the excellencies of English prose. English is a very difficult language to write. Its grammar is so complicated that even the best writers often make gross mistakes. The various influences to which it has been subjected have made it a difficult medium to handle. Pedants have burdened it with pomposities. Clowns have jumped with it through paper hoops and juggled with its beauties as though they were the properties of the circus ring. Rhetoricians have floundered in the richness of its vocabulary. But its excellencies remain unimpaired. It is with joy and pride that I can point to them in many of the authors who grace this collection by their works.

From:

Tellers of Tales

"Introduction"

(1939)

i

First of all I should like to tender my thanks to the various persons who have helped me to make this collection of short stories. They are Jacques de Lacretelle, of the French Academy, and Paul Morand; Dr. Carl Stransky, Bruno Frank and Stefan Zweig; Baroness Budberg, Graham Greene and Nella Henney. I must also declare my indebtedness to Fred Lewis Pattee whose book, *The Development of the American Short Story,* is invaluable to the student of this form of fiction.

ii

When I set about gathering material for this anthology it was with the ambitious aim of showing how the short story had developed since the beginning of the nineteenth century. My notion was to trace its evolution as the evolution of the horse may be traced from the tiny creature with five toes that ran about the forests of the Neocene period to the noble beast that, notwithstanding the mechanization of the age, still provides a decent living for bookmakers and tipsters. It is natural for men to tell tales, and I suppose the short story began in the night of time when the hunter, to beguile the leisure of his fellows when they had eaten and drunk their fill, narrated by the cavern fire some marvellous incident of

which he had heard. In cities of the East you can to this day
see the storyteller sitting in the market place, surrounded by
a circle of eager listeners, and hear him tell the tales that he
has inherited from an immemorial past. But I chose to start
with the nineteenth century because it was then that the
short story acquired a character and a currency that it had
not had before. Of course short stories had been written:
there were the religious stories of Greek origin, there were the
edifying narratives popular in the Middle Ages, and there
were the immortal stories of *The Thousand and One Nights;*
throughout the Renaissance, in Italy and Spain, in France
and England, there was a great vogue for brief narrative. The
Decameron of Boccaccio and the *Exemplary Tales* of Cervantes are its unperished monuments. But with the rise of
the novel the vogue dwindled. The booksellers would no
longer pay good money for a collection of short tales, and
the authors soon came to look askance on a form of fiction
that brought them neither profit nor renown. When from
time to time, conceiving a theme that they could adequately
treat in a little space, they wrote a short story, they did not
quite know what to do with it; and so, unwilling to waste it,
they inserted it, sometimes, one must admit, very clumsily,
into the body of their novels.

But at the beginning of the nineteenth century a new form
of publication was put before the reading public which very
soon acquired an immense popularity. The result shows that
the authors welcomed with delight the chance thus offered
to them for disposing to advantage of the brief pieces which
for one reason or another they had occasion to write. This
was the annual. It seems to have started in Germany. It was
a miscellany of prose and verse; and in its native land offered
its readers substantial fare, for we are told that Schiller's
Maid of Orleans and Goethe's *Hermann and Dorothea* first
appeared in periodicals of this character. But when their success led English publishers to imitate them they relied chiefly
on short stories to attract a sufficiency of readers. The an-

nual soon found its way to America and gave American authors an opportunity they had long been looking for.

iii

Now I must interrupt myself to tell the reader something
about literary composition of which, so far as I know, the
critics, whose duty it is doubtless to guide and instruct him,
have neglected to apprise him. The writer has in him the
desire to create, but he has also the desire to place before
readers the result of his labour and the desire (a harmless
one with which the reader is not concerned) to earn his
bread and butter. On the whole he finds it possible to direct
his creative gifts into the channels that will enable him to
satisfy these desires. At the risk of shocking the reader who
thinks the writer's inspiration should be uninfluenced by
practical considerations, I must further tell him that writers
quite naturally find themselves impelled to write the sort of
things for which there is a demand. When plays in verse
might bring an author fame and fortune it would probably
have been difficult to find a young man of literary bent who
had not among his papers a tragedy in five acts. I think it
would occur to few young men to write one now. Today
they write plays in prose, novels and short stories. The possibility of publication, the exigencies of editors, that is to say
their notion of what their readers want, have a great influence on the kind of work that at a particular time is produced. So, when magazines flourish which have room for
stories of considerable length, stories of that length are written; when on the other hand newspapers publish fiction, but
can give it no more than a small space, stories to fill that
space are supplied. There is nothing disgraceful in this. The
competent author can write a story in a couple of thousand
words as easily as he can write one in ten thousand. But he
chooses a different story or treats it in a different way. Guy de
Maupassant wrote one of his most celebrated tales, *The Leg-*

acy, twice over, once in a few hundred words for a newspaper and the second time in several thousand for a magazine; both are published in the collected edition of his works, and I think no one can read the two versions without admitting that in the first there is not a word too little and in the second not a word too much. The point I want to make is this: the nature of the vehicle whereby the writer approaches his public is one of the conventions he has to accept, and on the whole he finds that he can do this without any violence to his own inclinations.

Now at the beginning of the nineteenth century the annuals and keepsakes offered writers a means of introducing themselves to the public by way of the short story, and so short stories, serving a better purpose than merely to give a fillip to the reader's interest in the course of a long novel, began to be written in greater numbers than ever before. More especially was this the case in America where the lack of a copyright law made it difficult for American authors to find a publisher to publish their novels. English novels were pirated and the competition was too severe for the American author to meet; he was almost forced to write short stories, and fortunately for him, the public, which was content to read of foreign people and foreign scenes in novels, insisted in briefer narratives on native themes and native authors. Many hard things have been said of the annual and the lady's book, and harder things still of the magazine which succeeded them in the public favour; but it can scarcely be denied that the rich abundance of short stories that were produced in the nineteenth century was directly occasioned by the opportunity which these periodicals afforded. In America they gave rise to a school of writers so brilliant and so fertile that some persons, unacquainted with the history of literature, have claimed that the short story is an American invention. That is not so; but it may very well be admitted that in none of the countries of Europe has this form of fiction been so assiduously cultivated as it has been in the

United States; nor have its methods, technique and possibilities been elsewhere more attentively studied. The *North American Review* in 1829 looked upon the brief narrative as a literary toy and encouraged it only because it would prepare American authors 'for nobler and greater exertions.' But the event has proved that it could be an end in itself. Many writers have found in it so adequate a means of expression that they have been content to write nothing else. Nor need it be forgotten that the American short story has on more than one occasion profoundly influenced the practice of short-story writers in other countries.

iv

It did not seem unreasonable then, when I set out to show the development of the short story, to start with the nineteenth century. The first piece I chose was Sir Walter Scott's *The Two Drovers,* because it began my anthology with a great name and it had several qualities that I thought a good story should possess. But when I embarked upon the serious reading that my aim involved I made a most inconvenient discovery. I began with Washington Irving whose tales I had not read since I was a boy. He wrote them in a style which is now old-fashioned, and he had the mannerisms of his period; he did not attach importance, as have later authors, to the dramatic value of his theme, and he was inclined to talk, though very pleasantly, about his characters, rather than let them by dialogue and action disclose themselves; but when you have made allowances for all that, when you take them as stories apart from the telling, you can hardly fail to see how modern they really are. Of course Chekhov, if he had written *Rip Van Winkle,* would have written it very differently, but it is a story he might quite well have penned. The most astonishing thing in it is that the hero's strange experience has so little effect either on him or on the people of the village to which after his long sleep he returns. The incident is queer and affords a topic for the village gossip, but that is all. I think the truth and humour of this would have greatly pleased the Russian writer. And *The Stout Gentleman,* the second of Irving's tales that I have chosen for this collection, is as modern as it can be. Katherine Mansfield might easily have written it. I could not escape the conclusion that the short story which was written at the beginning of my period was as finished, well constructed, sophisticated and accomplished as any that were written during the last ten years.

When the nineteenth century was young, men had fewer ways of amusing their leisure than they have now and were not displeased if their fiction moved at a deliberate pace; they accepted without reluctance a dilatory exposition and a sauntering digressiveness. Writers still under the influence of the prose of Queen Anne wrote with greater elaboration than is now esteemed. Now everyone reads newspapers every day, one or more, and the reading public has grown to demand succinctness and a graphic way of putting things; the authors of short stories, newspaper readers themselves and often writers for the newspapers, have adopted the style that is in the air; and the elegant period of Washington Irving, the stately phrase of Hawthorne, are time-worn. But idiom changes; fashions come and go. The modern short story with its lack of ornament may well seem bare to a succeeding generation, and the colloquial manner which is the mode of the day may easily give way to a more formal style. The more I read the more was it forced upon my notice that in essentials the short story has changed little; what was a good story at the beginning of the nineteenth century is a good story today. I could not in face of this continue with the instructive intention with which I had started. I was obliged to relinquish my aim of showing the same sort of development in the brief narration as the biologist can show you in the development of the horse. It has been a disappointment to me. Notwithstanding, in the course of reading a vast number of stories written during the last century I have learnt a good deal about the form. It is this, and no more, that I can impart to the reader if he will have the patience to follow me through the remainder of this introduction.

v

I have had to abandon some of the notions I held before. The first of these concerns the nature of the short story. Now I should warn the reader at once that a writer treating of the art he pursues is biassed. He very naturally thinks his own practice best. He writes as he can, and as he must, because he is a certain sort of man; he has his own parts, and his own idiosyncrasy, so that he sees things in a manner peculiar to himself, and he gives his vision the form that is forced upon him by his nature. He requires a singular vigour of mind to sympathize with work that is antagonistic to all his instincts. One should be on one's guard when one reads a novelist's criticisms of other people's novels. He is apt to find that excellent which he is aiming at himself and he is likely to see little merit in qualities that he does not himself possess. One of the best books on the novel that has been published in recent years is by an admirable writer who has never in his life been able to devise a plausible story. I was not surprised to find that he held in small esteem the novelists whose great gift is that they can lend a thrilling verisimilitude to the events they relate. I do not blame him for this. Tolerance is a very good quality in a man: if it were commoner, the world of today would be a more agreeable place to live in than it is; but I am not so sure that it is so good in a writer. For what in the long run has the writer to give you? Himself. It is well that he should have breadth of vision, for life in all its extent is his province; but he must see it not only with his own eyes, he must apprehend it with his own nerves, his own heart and his own bowels; his knowledge is partial, of course, but it is distinct, because he is himself and not somebody else. His attitude is definite and characteristic. If he really feels that any other point of view is as valid as his own, he will hardly hold his own with energy and is unlikely to present it with force. It is commendable that a man should see that there are two sides to a question; but the writer face to face with the art he practises (and his view of life is of course part of his art) can only attain this standpoint by an effort of ratiocination: in his blood and his bones he feels that it is not six of one and half a dozen of the other, but twelve on his side and on the other zero. This unreasonableness would be most unfortunate if writers were few, or if the influence of one were so great as to compel the rest to conformity; but there are thousands of us. Each one of us has his little communication to make, a restricted one, and from all these communications the readers can choose, according to their own inclinations and their own experience of life, what suits them.

I have said all this to clear the ground. I like best the sort of story I can myself write. This is the sort of story that many people have written well, but no one more admirably than Maupassant, so I cannot do better, to show exactly what its nature is, than to discuss one of his most famous productions, *The Necklace*. At the base of it is an anecdote. It relates an incident which is curious, striking and original. But of course it is much more than an anecdote, for when you know this you can read the story with as much interest as before. The scene is set before you with brevity, as the medium requires, but with clearness; and the persons concerned, the kind of life they lead and their deterioration, are shown you with just the amount of detail that is needed to make the circumstances of the case plain. You are told everything that you should know about them. From this appears the second excellence of this sort of story; when you have read it to find out what happens you can read it again for the cleverness of the telling. *The Necklace* is not from its own standpoint perfect, for this kind of narrative should have a beginning, a middle and an end; and when the end is reached the whole story should have been told and you should neither wish nor need to ask a further question. Your crossword is filled up. But in this case Maupassant satisfied himself with an end that was ironic and effective. The practical reader can hardly fail to ask himself, what next? It is true that the unfortunate couple had lost their youth and most of what makes life pleasant in the dreary years they had passed saving money to pay for the lost necklace; but when they discovered that it was worthless they might very well have claimed the real one with which they had replaced it and then found themselves in possession of a small fortune. In the aridity of spirit to which their sacrifices had brought them, it might very well have seemed a satisfactory compensation. It is a tribute to Maupassant's skill that few readers remain so self-possessed that the objection occurs to them. This brings me to the third characteristic of this kind of story. The author does not copy life; he arranges it in order the better to interest, excite, and surprise. He demands from you a willing suspension of disbelief.

This has caused the sort of narrative with which I am now dealing to fall of late years into some discredit. People say that in real life things do not happen with this neatness; real life is an affair of broken threads and loose ends; to arrange them into a pattern falsifies. Such an author as Maupassant does not mind; he is not aiming at a transcription of life, but at a dramatization of it. He is willing to sacrifice plausibility to effect, and the test is whether he can get away with it: if he has so shaped the incidents he describes and the persons concerned in them that you are conscious of the violence he has put on them, he has failed. But that he sometimes fails is no argument against the method. I am disposed to think that the desire to tell stories and to listen to them is inherent in the human race. At some periods readers exact a close adherence to the facts of life as they know them—it is then that realism is in fashion; at others, indifferent to this, they ask for the strange, the unusual, the marvellous—these are periods that historians of literature call romantic; and then, so long as they are held, readers are willing to accept pretty well anything. They are willing to accept *Sinbad the Sailor* and *Monsieur Beaucaire*. In fiction probability changes with the inclinations of the time; it is what you can get your readers to swallow. No one has stated the canons of the kind of story which I am now discussing with more precision than Edgar Allan Poe. But for its length I would quote in full his review of Hawthorne's *Twice-Told Tales;* it says everything that is to be said on the matter. It is, however, so well known that I can content myself with a short extract.

A skilful literary artist has constructed a tale. If wise, he has not fashioned his thoughts to accommodate his incidents: but having conceived, with deliberate care, a certain unique or single effect to be brought out, he then invents such incidents—he then combines such effects as may best aid him in establishing this preconceived effect. If his very initial sentence tend not to the outbringing of this effect, then he has failed in his first step. In the whole composition there should be no word written, of which the tendency, direct or indirect, is not to the pre-established design. And by such means, with such care and skill, a picture is at length painted which leaves in the mind of him who contemplates it with a kindred art, a sense of the fullest satisfaction. The idea of the tale has been presented unblemished, because undisturbed. . . .

With this declaration to help one I think it is possible to frame a definition of what Poe meant by a good short story: it is a piece of fiction, dealing with a single incident, material or spiritual, that can be read at a sitting; it is original, it must sparkle, excite or impress; and it must have unity of effect or impression. It should move in an even line from its exposition to its close.

vi

But as I continued to read, I could not but grow conscious of the fact that there are a great many excellent stories which by these canons would have to be condemned. Now the critic does not prescribe laws for the artist; he takes note of his common practice and from this deduces rules; but when an original talent breaks them, the critic, though he may jib like the devil, in the end is forced to change his rules to accommodate the novelty. It is evident that there are other ways than Poe's of writing a good story.

People grow tired even of good things. They want change. To take an example from another art: domestic architecture during the Georgian Era reached a rare perfection; the houses that were built then were good to look at and comfortable to live in. The rooms were spacious, airy and well proportioned. You would have thought people would be content with such houses for ever. But no. The romantic era approached; they wanted the quaint, the fanciful and the picturesque; and the architects, not unwilling, built them what they wanted. It is hard to invent such a story as Poe wrote and, as we know, even he, in his small output, more than once repeated himself. There is a good deal of trickiness in a narrative of this kind, and when, with the appearance and immediate popularity of the monthly magazine, the demand for such narratives became great, authors were not slow to learn the tricks. Craftsmen rather than artists, in order to make their stories effective they forced upon them a conventional design and presently deviated so far from plausibility in their delineation of life that their readers rebelled. They grew weary of stories written to a pattern they knew only too well. They demanded greater realism. Now to copy life has never been the artist's business. If you look at the painting and sculpture of the past you cannot but be surprised to see how little the great artists have occupied themselves with an exact rendering of what they saw before them. We are apt to think that the distortions of the plastic artists have imposed upon their materials, best illustrated in the cubists of yesterday, are an invention of our own times. That is not so. From the beginnings of Western painting artists have sacrificed verisimilitude to the effects they sought. If El Greco gave an extravagant length to the figures he painted, it was surely not because he thought human beings, even though saintly, looked like that, but because he wanted to get on canvas an idea in his mind's eye. It is the same with fiction. Not to go far back, take Poe; it is incredible that he should have thought human beings spoke in the way he made his characters speak: if he put into their mouths dialogue that seems to us so unreal, it must be because he thought it suited the kind of story he was telling and helped him to achieve the deliberate purpose which we know he had in view. Artists have only affected naturalism when it was borne in upon them that they had gone so far from life that a return was necessary, and then they have set themselves to copy it as exactly as they could, not as an end in itself, but as a salutary discipline.

In the short story naturalism in the nineteenth century came into fashion in reaction to a romanticism that had become tedious. One after the other writers attempted to portray life with unflinching veracity. 'I have never truckled,' said Frank Norris, 'I never took off the hat to fashion and held it out for pennies. By God! I told them the Truth. They liked it or they didn't like it. What had that to do with me? I told them the Truth, I knew it for the Truth then, and I know it for the Truth now.' (These are brave words. But it is hard to tell what the truth is; it is not necessarily the opposite of what you know to be a lie.) Writers of this school looked upon life with less partial eyes than those of the generation that had preceded them; they were less sugary and less optimistic, more violent and more direct; their dialogue was more natural and they chose their characters from a world that since the days of Defoe writers of fiction had somewhat neglected; but they made no innovations in technique. So far as the essentials of the short story are concerned they were content with the old models. The effects they pursued were still those that had been pursued by Poe; they used the formula he had laid down. Their merit proves its value; their artificiality exposes its weakness.

But there was a country in which the formula had little prevailed. In Russia they had been writing for a couple of generations stories of quite another order; and when the fact forced itself upon the attention both of readers and of authors that the kind of story that had so long found favour was grown tediously mechanical, it was discovered that in that country there was a body of writers who had made of the short story something new and vital. I would not offer it as a dogmatic statement but merely as a suggestion that the inventor of the Russian story as we know it was Tolstoy. In *The Death of Iván Ilých,* which the reader will find in this volume, there is a great deal more than the germ of all the Russian stories that have been written since. It comprehends all the merits and all the defects of the Russian story.

It is singular that it took so long for this variety of the brief narrative, not to reach the Western world, for the stories of Turgenev were read in French translations when the Goncourts were writing their *Journal,* but to have any effect on it. About 1905 I was in Paris, where Arnold Bennett was then living. He was widely read in modern literature and was always alert for anything new within the field of his interests. He knew the work of Tolstoy and Turgenev, and his admiration for it, though discriminating, was great; but I do not think that he found in it anything that was personally important to him as a writer. It was another matter when he read Chekhov; in him he found something that very definitely affected him. A writer of short stories himself, he saw in the Russian's impressive achievement new life for an exhausted form. Since then the prestige of the Russian writers in gen-

eral and of Chekhov in particular, has been immense. It has
to a large extent transformed the composition and the appreciation of short stories. Critical readers turn away with
indifference from the story which is technically known as well
made, and the writers who produce it still, for the delectation
of the great mass of the public, are little considered. The
stories that Maupassant wrote in France, Rudyard Kipling in
England, and Bret Harte in America have come to be regarded with some disdain.

vii

To write a story in accordance with the principles laid
down by Edgar Allan Poe is not so easy as some think. It
requires intelligence, not perhaps of a very high order, but
of a special kind; it requires a sense of form and no small
power of invention. But it is plain that this manner of story
no longer carries conviction. The modern story fulfills a
spiritual need in the modern reader which the old story
cannot satisfy. The technique and the outlook of the writers
of today differ a good deal from those of the masters of the
nineteenth century; but before I go into this I must mention
a circumstance that has forced itself upon my attention and
that has caused me a certain perplexity; this is that so many
of these stories might have been written by the same hand.
It looks as though there were something in the method of the
modern short story that submerges the personality of the
author. The stories of Henry James, of Maupassant and of
Chekhov could only have been written by themselves. You
may not like the personality of these authors, but there it is,
manifest to the grossest sense, in their every page. For my
part I have always thought that just this, the personality of
the creator, was what gave a work of art its lasting interest;
it does not matter if it is a slightly absurd one, as with Henry
James, a somewhat vulgar one, as with Maupassant, or a
grey, melancholic one, as with Chekhov: so long as he can

present it, distinct and idiosyncratic, his work has life. The short-story writers of our time seem to lack this curious power. Violent though they often are, hard, ruthless and devoid of sentimentality, they seldom manage to impress their special individuality upon their work. They are communal writers. They remind one of the decorative painters in the eighteenth century who painted flower pieces to put over doors or let into panels above the chimneypiece; it is a pleasant art, but its merit owes more to a period than to a personal gift.

The writers of the present time, unless I am mistaken, are more interested in social circumstances, in the injustice of modern conditions, in the relation of persons to their environment, in short, than in their relations to one another. The result of this is that they are likely to suffer from a certain shortage of material. If you know all about a sawmill, for instance, if you have yourself worked in one, you can probably write a very good story about it, even two or three; but you cannot go on writing stories about sawmills indefinitely; presently you will have said all you can on the subject, and then you are obliged to look for some other environment. You are lucky if you can find one about which you can learn to write with first-hand knowledge. It is a grave handicap that these specialist writers, of which there are so many nowadays, labour under; they exhaust their subjects, and, as we know, either go on writing the same old story to the weariness of their readers, or lapse into silence. The only subject that is inexhaustible is man. You can go on writing all your life and touch no more than the fringe of it. The difficulty of the writer who eschews a plot—and a plot, I should add, is no more than the pattern that is imposed upon the conduct of the various persons with whom you are dealing—in favour of a narration of the circumstances offered by a certain environment is that, getting nearer and nearer to life as we know it is lived, avoiding surprise, thrill, unexpected yet logical accident, which are the essential characteristics of the formal story, he has nothing to offer the reader that the narrator of actual facts cannot give him with greater force. He has ceased to be a writer of fiction; he has become a reporter. To prove this point I have printed at the end of this anthology a piece from a collection of true accounts of events written by the persons who took part in them. They are so good, so complete, so vivid that the candid reader can hardly fail to admit that they are as well worth reading as many short stories. And the fact that he knows they are true gives them an added point.

It is the death of the short story if it can be beaten at its own game by the naked truth. If the short story is to be a work of art it must be more than that. It will not do to say that the storyteller selects. The writers of this volume of true stories (it is called *Life in the United States* and is published by Scribners) have also selected: from the mass of their experience they have taken occasions that seemed to them significant and their attitude towards life has influenced their choice. They too have had an emotional reaction to the circumstances they describe. It happens to be a different one from those that chiefly affect modern writers, but I cannot bring myself to think it less admirable. It is fortitude. Modern writers are mostly moved by pity and anger; indeed pity is the fashionable literary emotion of our day. It is that for which a novelist is most praised. Critics have even found it in Chekhov, though the readers of his own time often complained that his objectivity was such that you could not tell from his stories where his sympathies lay. Now everyone knows that the world is in a bad way, liberty is dead or dying, poverty, relentless exploitation of labour, cruelty, injustice are everywhere. There is good cause for anger and pity; but they are unprofitable emotions unless they lead you to some effort. They are despicable when, satisfied that you have the generosity to feel them, you will not get busy to change the conditions that have aroused them. It is not for nothing that the tender Spinoza called pity womanish. In our small contemporary world of writers and readers it is too often a balm we apply to our wounded souls in order that we may spare ourselves the inconvenience of action. The writer's business is not to pity, nor to rage, but to understand.

viii

At the beginning of this introduction I called the reader's attention to the fact that writers are more likely to write stories when they can get a public for them. The great flowering of the art during the nineteenth century is due to the popularity of the magazines. As we know, they began to prosper round about the forties and their success finally killed the decaying annuals and keepsakes which at an earlier period had given writers their only opportunity. I suppose that this success reached its culmination during the first third of the present century. Never was there a greater demand for short stories, never were higher prices paid for them, and never was there a larger number of writers to write them. But the vogue of the magazine, I suspect, is waning. People spend an increasing part of their leisure in athletic exercises, they golf, play tennis, motor and swim; they have the cinema to go to and the gramophone to listen to; they have the radio. Cheaper and cheaper books, of a size convenient for the pocket, offer reading matter that more satisfactorily supplies present needs. One can hardly suppose that the magazines will be displaced by some other form of periodical as the magazines displaced the annuals that once flourished so luxuriantly, but it is at least not unlikely that the magazines will change their character and so cease to offer an outlet to the writer of short stories. Already editors, disturbed by their falling circulations and thinking that in the distressed condition of the world their readers demand more solid fare than fiction, are giving more space to articles of an informative character. But I cannot believe that people will lose their desire to listen to stories. As I said before, that seems to me a desire inherent in the human race. It is not my business to prophesy, the world is sufficiently full of prophets, mostly, I am afraid, of evil; but it is at least not absurd to suggest that this need may well be satisfied by the radio. It may be that listeners will take the place of readers and that those who want the entertainment of the short story will be content to hear it over the air. Then the art will have gone full circle. The short story started with the tale told by the hunter round the fire in the cave which was the dwelling of primitive man, and, having run its long long course, will then return to its origins. The teller of tales, sitting before his microphone, will narrate his story to an immense crowd of unseen listeners.

But if this happens it is hard to believe that he will have an attentive audience if he tells stories that depend on atmosphere, if he tells stories that are sketchy or digressive, stories of implication, or stories whose meaning is obscure. One can but suppose that his stories will have to be direct, gripping, surprising and dramatic. They will have to move swiftly in one unbroken line from the beginning that arouses interest to the end that satisfies the curiosity that has been excited. They will in a word have to resemble more closely the stories of Maupassant than the stories of Chekhov. But that is not yet. Tolstoy, Chekhov and many another writer either influenced by them or, like Sherwood Anderson, arriving at a similar form by native idiosyncrasy, have enriched literature with a number of pieces the merit of which is great; and if these compositions will not fit into the definition of a short story which may be deduced from the formula so well stated by Poe, then the definition must be changed to include them. I would now offer a very simple one. I should define a short story as a piece of fiction that has unity of impression and that can be read at a single sitting. I should be inclined to say that the only test of its excellence is that it interests. It is with this principle in mind that I have chosen the stories in this volume.

ix

There is a certain amount of fiction that it becomes every well-bred man to have read; it belongs to the culture of the world, and so far as culture is a part of knowledge it must be regarded as essential to everyone's education. But there is not much of it. I think a bookcase that held twenty books would be large enough to contain all the works of fiction that it would leave a man spiritually poorer not to have read. This bookcase would contain *Don Quixote, Wilhelm Meister, Pride and Prejudice, Le Rouge et le Noir, Le Père Goriot, Madame Bovary, War and Peace, David Copperfield, The Brothers Karamazov* and *A la Recherche du Temps Perdu;* but I am not sure that it would contain any short stories. For the short story is a minor art, and it must content itself with moving, exciting and amusing the reader. There are a hundred stories in this book, and I do not think there is a single one that will fail to do at least one of these things, but also I do not think that there is any that will give the reader that thrill, that rapture, that fruitful energy which great art can produce. The most important short-story writers of the nineteenth century were not men who had it in them to achieve such effects. They had talent and they were artists; but Maupassant had some commonness in his nature, and Henry James, who took his calling with such an admirable seriousness, was defeated by a peculiar triviality of soul; Chekhov was neither trivial nor common, but as is evident when on occasion he indulges in general reflection, his mental capacity was mediocre. None of these writers impresses you by the power and fullness of his personality as you are impressed when you read Balzac or Tolstoy.

It is wise then to read short stories for the entertainment they provide. It is unreasonable to ask of them more than they can give you. But it would be foolish to despise them on that account.

X

But entertainment is a personal thing. Just as there is no obligation to read fiction there is no obligation to like it. The critics often try to browbeat us plain men by telling us that we ought to like this, that and the other, and they call us hard names if we will not do as they bid. There is no ought in the matter. The critic can point out the excellences he sees, and since they may have escaped your attention, in this he does you a service; but when he condemns you because you do not care for the work he admires he is foolish. The history of criticism shows that critics are often mistaken. The only thing that really matters to you is what a work of art says to you. Even if the consensus of educated opinion is against you, you should be unperturbed. However great a work is commonly agreed to be, if it bores you, to read it is futile; it must entertain *you*, or so far as you are concerned it is valueless.

It is on this principle that I have chosen the stories in this volume. I have been influenced neither by the reputation nor by the common opinion that ascribed them merit. These stories are stories I like. I cannot hope that all my readers will like them all. To do so they would have had to have my particular experience of life and to share my prejudices and my interests. I do not claim that they are the best stories that have been written during the last century; they are the stories amongst all those that I have read that have interested me most.

When my reading forced me to broaden my definition of a short story so that it included almost anything approaching fiction that was not of excessive length, I was able to insert a number of pieces that, if I had adhered to Poe's canon, I should have felt bound to omit. I was able to put in Flaubert's *A Simple Heart*, which he himself called a short story, but which is really a short novel. Such unity of impression as it has depends only on the fact that the interest is concentrated on a single person. But it is only as short as it is and no longer, because in comparatively few pages Flaubert was able to say all there was to say about the straightforward, limited character he set out to describe. It is a moving tale, and it is somewhat important in the history of fiction because it has given rise to numberless studies, sometimes in the form of the short story, sometimes in that of the novel, of women of the servant class. It is besides a story which, I think, no one can read without gaining a sympathetic understanding of the French nature, with its great virtues and pardonable failings; for all France is there. This looseness of definition has also made it possible for me to put in Joseph Conrad's excellent *Typhoon* rather than one of his briefer pieces. Conrad rarely wrote anything but short stories, though, being a writer of an exuberant verbosity, he often made them as long as most novels. He needed sea-room. He had little sense of concision. A theme with him was like the stem of a cauliflower; it grew and grew under his active pen until, all its branches headed with succulent flowers, it became a very fine but somewhat monstrous plant. *Typhoon* shows all his power and none of his weakness. It is a tale of the sea, which he knew better than he knew the land, and it is concerned with men, whom he knew better than he knew women. These sailor chaps are a little simpler than most of us now think human beings really are, but they live. *Typhoon* narrates an incident, which was a thing Conrad could do with mastery, and the subject gives him opportunity for his wonderful and vivid descriptions of the phenomena of nature. My final definition has even allowed me to adorn my pages with E. M. Forster's *Mr. and Mrs. Abbey's Difficulties,* which is a little bit of literary history written in the guise of fiction; it has a surprise ending that would have delighted the mind of O. Henry. It is a moving and exquisite piece, written in such admirable English that it might well find a place in any manual for teaching the language.

xi

When I abandoned my ambitious project of showing the development of the short story from the beginning of the nineteenth century, I was able to do something that caused me a considerable measure of relief. I was able, to wit, to omit a number of stories that under my original scheme I should have had to insert. There are few works of art that preserve their vitality from age to age. Even they have their ups and downs. For long periods they lie comatose like hibernating animals, and then, as a new generation finds something in them to satisfy its new wants, they take on a new lease of life. Thus, the archaic sculpture of Greece, the paintings of the school of Siena, after being neglected for a long period, in our own day, with its relish for the primitive, its taste for suggestion rather than for downright statement, have been found to possess a troubling beauty that corresponds to our high-strung needs as does neither the resolute achievement of Phidias nor the opulent splendour of Titian. And in literature when romanticism, fired by the discovery of the Middle Ages, rejected the measure and reason of the eighteenth century, when the sensitiveness of the human soul first recoiled from the mechanization of life, writers found inspiration and readers refreshment in books like Malory's *Morte d'Arthur* and Froissart's *Chronicles*.

But there are many works of art that live their lives and die. They have had something to say to the generation that saw their birth, but with the passing of that generation lose their import. They may still have an interest for the student or the historian, but they are no longer works of art. They can no longer give its specific thrill. They have had a long and honourable career, and there is no cause for their authors to turn uneasily in their graves; they have fulfilled their purpose and may now rest in peace. But I have not wished any of the stories in this collection to be looked upon as museum pieces. I have inserted nothing that does not seem to me to have a living interest. That is why I have chosen mostly stories that are contemporary, or almost so. I dare say that in fifty years many of them will seem as old-fashioned as the stories of fifty years ago that I have discarded. That is not my affair. Now they have the merit of actuality. It is this merit that enables us to compete with the great authors of the past. Otherwise who would read us? The bad, the mediocre, have long since been forgotten and only the best has remained. Who would bother to read a modern novel if *Roxana, Tom Jones* and *Middlemarch* had just that appeal that we can give to our works because we can dress our characters in the clothes of today and make them speak the language of our time?

I hesitated a good deal when I considered the tales of Nathaniel Hawthorne. He was a distinguished and important writer of short stories, and he had a considerable influence both on his contemporaries and on his successors. I read him and reread him. It seemed to me that his stories had lost the life they once assuredly had. In order to find an interest in them now, one has to bethink oneself of the circumstances of his life, the period he lived in and the effect on him of the romantic revival which at the time swept Europe like a tidal wave. Historians of literature claim that *Rappacini's Daughter* is a masterpiece. To me it seems stuff and nonsense. I am only too willing to suspend my disbelief, but that is a mouthful that I really cannot swallow. I think the story of Hawthorne's that has most life in it today is *The Artist of the Beautiful,* for that is the story of every creator in relation to his creation and to the world without; it is universal, but alas, so diffuse and so repetitive that its power is sadly diminished. To my mind Hawthorne's best story is the story of his own life, and that you may read in that enchanting book, *The Flowering of New England,* by Van Wyck Brooks. It is on account of this that I could not bring myself to omit Hawthorne from this anthology, and so I have chosen *The*

Gray Champion. It has thrill and is informed with a noble
patriotism which you will have to hunt far and wide to find
represented in the short story. Now that liberty in so many
quarters of the world is immured and fettered, it is more
than ever necessary to cherish an expression of its beauty.

I had no such hesitations when I came to read the stories
that depended for their interest on local colour and dialect.
Their vogue started in the seventies and lasted for many
years. The manner reached its greatest excellence in the
work of Mary Wilkins Freeman. She had grace, feeling and
sincerity. I am sure her stories were very good in their day,
but their day is past; the sun has faded their delicate tints
and they are now somewhat namby-pamby. It is the namby-
pamby which till quite recently has been the bane of the
English short story. This failing has made it difficult for me
to find any stories written in the last third of the century in
England that seemed to me to have merit. The writers of that
period were gentle, urbane and sentimental. They closed
their eyes to such aspects of life as they did not wish to see.
English writers on the whole have not taken kindly to the
art of the short story. They have felt the novel more con-
genial to their idiosyncrasy, for the English, though in conversation often tongue-tied, when they take a pen in their
hands are inclined to prolixity. They have no natural instinct for succinctness, which is indispensable to the short
story, nor a sense of form, which is essential to its significance. So the diffuseness of the national temper has found its
most satisfactory literary expression in the long, unwieldy,
shapeless novels of the Victorian Era which still remain the
country's outstanding contribution to the world's fiction.
English writers find it difficult to be brief without being
trivial, and for the most part they have looked upon the short
story as a thing of no great matter to be thrown off in their
spare time in order to earn a few useful guineas without
much expenditure of effort. I know only two English writers
who have taken the short story as seriously as it must be

taken if excellence is to be achieved, Rudyard Kipling, namely, and Katherine Mansfield. Miss Mansfield had a small, derivative, but exquisite talent; and her shorter pieces —for she had insufficient power to deal with a theme that demanded a sold gift of construction—are admirable. Rudyard Kipling stands in a different category. He alone among English writers of the short story can bear comparison with the masters of France and Russia.

Though Rudyard Kipling captured the attention of the public when first he began to write, and has retained a firm hold on it ever since, there was a time when educated opinion was somewhat disdainful of him. He was identified with an imperialism which events made obnoxious to many sensible persons. Certain characteristics of his style, which at first had seemed fresh and amusing, became irksome to readers of fastidious taste. But that time is past. I think there would be few now to deny that he was a wonderful, varied and original teller of tales. He had a fertile invention and to a supreme degree the gift of narrating incident in a surprising and dramatic fashion. His influence for a while was great on his fellow-writers, but perhaps greater on his fellow-men, who led in one way or another the sort of life he dealt with. When one travelled in the East it was astonishing how often one came across men who had modelled themselves on the creatures of his fancy. Critics say that Balzac's characters were more true of the generation that followed him than of that which he purported to describe; I know from my own experience that twenty years after Kipling wrote his first important stories there were men scattered about the outlying parts of the world who would never have been just what they were if he had not written them. He not only created characters, he created men. Rudyard Kipling is generally supposed to have rendered the British people conscious of their Empire, but that is a political achievement with which I have not here to deal; what is significant to my present standpoint is that in his discovery of the exotic story he opened a new and fruitful field to writers. This is the story, the scene of which is set in some country little known to the majority of readers, and which deals with the reactions upon the white man of his sojourn in an alien land and the effect which contact with peoples of another race has upon him. Subsequent writers have treated this subject in their different ways, but Rudyard Kipling was the first to blaze the trail through this new-found country, and no one has invested it with a more romantic glamour, no one has made it more exciting and no one has presented it so vividly and with such a wealth of colour. He wrote many stories of other kinds, but none in my opinion which surpassed these. He had, like every writer that ever lived, his shortcomings, but remains notwithstanding the best short-story writer that England can boast of.

xii

Now I wish to speak of Henry James. Greatness is a quality which is loosely ascribed to writers, and it is well to be cautious in one's use of the word, but I think no one will quarrel with me when I say that Henry James is the most distinguished literary figure that America has produced. He was a voluminous writer of short stories. Though he lived so long in England, and indeed in the end was naturalized, he remained an American to the last. I cannot feel that he ever knew the English as an Englishman instinctively knows them, and for that reason I have chosen for this book an American, rather than an English, story. The characters ring more true to life; his English people are more Jamesian than English.

It is impossible, I imagine, for anyone who knew Henry James in the flesh to read his stories dispassionately. He got the sound of his voice into every line he wrote, and you accept the convoluted style of his later work, his long-windedness and his mannerisms, because they are part and parcel of the charm, benignity and amusing pomposity of the man you remember. He was, if not a great, a remarkable man, so the reader will perhaps forgive me if in what follows I do not confine myself precisely to the consideration of his stories, which in this introduction is my only concern. The number of persons who knew him is growing smaller year by year, and such recollections of him as they have must be worth preservation. I do not foresee that I shall ever have a more suitable occasion than this to put my own on record. I knew Henry James for many years, but I was never more than an acquaintance of his. I am not sure that he was fortunate in his friends. They were disposed to be possessive, and they regarded one author's claim to be in the inner circle of his confidence with no conspicuous amiability. Like a dog with a bone, each was inclined to growl when another showed an inclination to dispute his exclusive right to the precious object of his admiration. The reverence with which they treated him was of no great service to him. They seemed to me, indeed, sometimes a trifle silly: they whispered to one another with delighted giggles that Henry James privately stated that the article in *The Ambassador* the nature of which he had left in polite obscurity and on whose manufacture the fortune of the widow Newsome was founded, was in fact a chamber pot. I did not find this so amusing as they did. But I must admit I was often doubtful of the quality of Henry James's humour. When someone transplants himself from his own country to another he is more likely to assimilate the defects of its inhabitants than their virtues. The England in which Henry James lived was excessively class-conscious and I think it is to this that must be ascribed the somewhat disconcerting attitude that he adopted in his writings to those who were so unfortunate as to be of humble origin. Unless he were an artist, by choice a writer, it seemed to him more than a little ridiculous that anyone should be under the necessity of earning his living. The death of a member of the lower classes could be trusted to give him a good chuckle.

I think this attitude was emphasized by the fact that, himself
of exalted lineage, he could not have dwelt long in England
without becoming aware that to the English one American
was very like another. He saw compatriots, on the strength
of a fortune acquired in Michigan or Ohio, received with
as great cordiality as though they belonged to the eminent
families of Boston and New York; and in self-defense somewhat exaggerated his native fastidiousness in social relations.
I think it should be added that perhaps in England his more
intimate associations were with persons who were not, to use
the vulgar phrase, out of the top drawer; but out of a drawer
just below. Their own position was not so secure that they
could ignore it.

Two of my meetings with Henry James stand out in my
memory. One was in London at a performance of a Russian
play by the Stage Society. I think it must have been *The
Cherry Orchard*, but after so many years I cannot be
certain. It was very badly acted. I found myself sitting with
Henry James and Mrs. Clifford, the widow of a celebrated
mathematician and herself a well-known novelist; and we
could none of us make head or tail of it. The intervals were
long, and there was ample opportunity for conversation. The
play disconcerted Henry James, and he set out to explain to
us how antagonistic to his French sympathies was this Russian incoherence. Lumbering through his tortuous phrases,
he hesitated now and again in search of the exact word to express his dismay; but Mrs. Clifford had a quick and agile
mind, she knew the word he was looking for and every time
he paused immediately supplied it. But this was the last thing
he wanted. He was too well mannered to protest, but an
almost imperceptible expression on his face betrayed his irri-
tation, and obstinately refusing the word she offered, he
laboriously sought another. The climax came when they began to discuss the actress who was playing the leading part.
Henry James wanted to know to what class she belonged, and
both Mrs. Clifford and I knew exactly what in plain terms he

wished to say. But that, he thought, would be tasteless, and so he wrapped up his meaning in an increasingly embarrassed flow of circumlocution till at last Mrs. Clifford could bear it no longer and blurted out: 'Do you mean, is she a lady?' A look of real suffering crossed his face. Put so, the question had a vulgarity that outraged him. He pretended not to hear. He made a little gesture of desperation and said: 'Is she, *enfin*, what you'd call, if you were asked point-blank, if you were put with your back to the wall, is she a *femme du monde?*'

The second occasion I remember is when Henry James, his brother William having recently died, was staying at Cambridge, Massachusetts, with his sister-in-law. I happened to be in Boston, and Mrs. James asked me to dinner. There were but the three of us; I can remember nothing of the conversation at table, but it seemed to me that Henry James was troubled in spirit; after dinner the widow left us alone in the dining room, and he told me that he had promised his brother to stay at Cambridge for, I think, six months after his death, so that if he found himself able to make a communication from beyond the grave there would be two sympathetic witnesses on the spot ready to receive it. I could not but reflect that Henry James was in such a state of nervousness that it would be difficult to place implicit confidence in any report he might make. His sensibility was so exasperated that he was capable of imagining anything. But hitherto no message had come, and the six months were drawing to their end.

When it was time for me to go, Henry James insisted on accompanying me to the corner where I could take the street-car back to Boston. I protested that I was perfectly capable of getting there by myself, but he would not hear of it; this not only on account of the kindness and the great courtesy that were natural to him, but also because America seemed to him a strange and terrifying labyrinth in which without his guidance I was bound to get hopelessly lost. When we were

on the way, by ourselves, he told me what his good manners
had prevented him from saying before Mrs. James, that he
was counting the days that must elapse before, having fulfilled his promise, he could sail for the blessed shores of
England. He yearned for it. There in Cambridge he felt himself forlorn. He was determined never again to set foot
on the bewildering and unknown country that America was
to him. It was then that he uttered the phrase which seemed
to me so fantastic that I have always remembered it. 'I
wander about those great empty streets of Boston,' he said,
'and I never see a living creature. I could not be more alone
in the Sahara.' The streetcar hove in sight and Henry James
was seized with agitation. He began waving frantically when
it was still a quarter of a mile away. He was afraid it wouldn't
stop, and he besought me to jump on with the greatest
agility of which I was capable, for it would not pause for
more than an instant, and if I were not very careful I might
be dragged along, and if not killed, at least mangled and
dismembered. I assured him that I was quite accustomed
to getting on streetcars. Not American streetcars, he told me;
they were of a savagery, an inhumanity, a ruthlessness beyond any conception. I was so infected by his anxiety that
when the car pulled up and I leapt on, I had almost the
sensation that I had had a miraculous escape from a fearful
death. I saw him standing on his short legs in the middle of
the road, looking after the car, and I felt that he was trem-
bling still at my narrow shave.

When for this book I read, yet once again, the short stories
of Henry James, I was troubled by the contrast offered by the
triviality of so many of his themes and the elaboration of
his treatment. He seems to have had no inkling that his
subject might be too slight to justify so intricate a method.
This is a fault that lessens one's enjoyment of some of his most
famous tales. A world that has gone through the great war,
that has lived through the troubled years that have followed
it, can hardly fail to be impatient with events, persons and

subtleties that seem so remote from life. Henry James had discernment, a generous heart and artistic integrity; but he applied his gifts to matters of no great import. He was like a man who should provide himself with all the impedimenta necessary to ascend Mount Everest in order to climb Primrose Hill. Let us not forget that here was a novelist who had to his hand one of the most stupendous subjects that any writer ever had the chance of dealing with, the rise of the United States from the small, provincial country that he knew in his youth to the vast and powerful commonwealth that it has become; and he turned his back on it to write about tea parties in Mayfair and country-house visits in the home shires. The great novelists, even in seclusion, have lived life passionately; Henry James was content to observe it from a window. But you cannot describe life unless you have partaken of it; nor, should your object be different, can you fantasticate upon it (as Balzac and Dickens did) unless you know it first. Something escapes you unless you have been an actor in the tragicomedy. Henry James was shy of the elementals of human nature. His heart was an organ subject to no serious agitation, and his interests were confined to persons of his own class. He failed of being a very great writer because his experience was inadequate and his sympathies were imperfect.

xiii

Now I have little more to say. I have limited myself in this anthology to five countries, France, Germany, Russia, England and the United States. Scandinavia, Denmark especially, has produced stories of uncommon merit, and Italy, too, has several writers who should find a place in any anthology; but if I had inserted them, there seemed no reason why I should leave out Spain, Hungary, and half a dozen more. It would have made this book unwieldy. None of these countries, moreover, has produced the immense body of work that has been produced in the five countries from which I have chosen; nor has any of them (with the exception of Denmark with Hans Andersen) produced anything that could not be paralleled in them. At one time I used to buy modern pictures, and Rosenberg, the dealer, said to me: don't bother with any but the *chefs d'école;* their followers may have merits, but in the long run it is only the leaders that count. So far as short stories are concerned the *chefs d'école* are to be found in the countries whose works are represented in this volume.

The reader who glances at the table of contents will notice that I have chosen more stories from England and America than from France and Russia and Germany. This is not because I think they are better, but because the book is designed for American and English readers, and to them stories of their own writers will, I imagine, prove more interesting. Besides, however well a story is translated, it loses something in the process; it can never have the flavour it had and so it is not quite so good as it was in its own language. I have arranged the stories roughly in chronological order, but not so strictly as to prevent me from putting them in the order in which I thought they could be most agreeably read. I have sought to balance matter and manner, the serious and the gay, the short and the long, so that the reader should be led from story to story without tedium. I have mixed up the various countries in such a manner as I have thought would help me in this. The exception I have made is in the case of Russia. Russian stories are so singular, they have on the whole so slender a connection with occidental culture, that I feel they must be taken by themselves. One has to shift one's outlook on life, one's feelings on all manner of things, on to another plane, as it were, in order to get into a suitable relation with their authors. I have chosen those printed in this volume because there was in them at least some glimmering of form; but more particularly because they give a picture of an experiment in civilization to which none of us who have to live for some little time yet on this earth can be indifferent. Their authors are Soviet authors, now living in Russia; the lack of skill shown by most of them gives their stories a convincing character which, if they had known their business, might not have been so apparent. To my mind they show very strikingly how men and women have been living together in Russia in the recent past and how the conditions of existence have affected their attitude towards the elemental things of life and love and death which are the essential materials not only of poetry but of fiction. I should like to point out that in the humorous story called *The Knives,* the reader will find one that might have been written in any country in the world. It is foolish to generalize on a single instance, but this suggests to me that humour has a universal quality, so that it is at least possible that if it were more generally exercised among the nations there is a chance that the differences dividing us, and the discords that afflict us, might be in some measure mitigated.

Now I have but one more thing to say. I have left out stories by certain living writers who hold an honourable position in the world of letters. I have done so because I do not myself happen to like them. Their authors, should they chance to glance over this book, would be wrong to be offended with me. We can none of us expect to be liked by everybody, and when we realize that somebody has no fancy for us, we may be curious to know why but we have no right to be angry. There are doubtless excellent stories by writers of perhaps considerable talent that do not chance to please me. That does not in the least affect their merit. I would never claim that my taste is perfect; all I can claim is that in making such a selection as this the anthologist's taste is the only standard.

From:

Maugham's Choice of Kipling's Best

"THE FINEST STORY
  IN THE WORLD"
THE MAN WHO WAS
THE TOMB OF HIS
  ANCESTORS
AT THE END OF
  THE PASSAGE
"WIRELESS"
ON GREENHOW HILL
"LOVE-O'-WOMEN"
THE BRUSHWOOD
  BOY
THE MAN WHO
  WOULD BE KING

WILLIAM THE
  CONQUEROR
"THEY"
TODS' AMENDMENT
MOWGLI'S BROTHERS
THE MIRACLE OF
  PURUN BHAGAT
WITHOUT BENEFIT
  OF CLERGY
THE VILLAGE THAT
  VOTED THE EARTH
  WAS FLAT

In this essay it is my business to deal only with Rudyard Kipling's short stories. I am not concerned with his verse nor, except in so far as they sometimes directly affected his stories, with his political opinions.

In making a selection of them I have had to decide whether I should choose only those I most liked. In that case I should have chosen nearly all the Indian stories. For in them to my mind he was at his best. When he wrote stories about Indians and about the British in India he felt himself at home and he wrote with an ease, a freedom, a variety of invention which gave them a quality which in stories in which the subject matter was different he did not always attain. Even the slightest of them are readable. They give you the tang of the East, the smell of the bazaars, the torpor of the rains, the heat of the sun-scorched earth, the rough life of the barracks in which the occupying troops were quartered, and the other life, so English and yet so alien to the English way, led by the officers, the Indian Civilians and the swarm of minor officials who combined to administer that vast territory.

A great many years ago, when Kipling was still at the height of his popularity, I used sometimes to meet Indian Civilians and professors at Indian universities who spoke of him with something very like contempt. That was partly due to an ignoble but natural jealousy. They resented it that this obscure journalist, of no social consequence, should have achieved world-wide renown. They protested that he did not know India. Which of them did? India is not a country, it is a continent. It is true that Kipling seems to have been intimately acquainted only with the North-West. Like any other sensible writer he placed the scene of his stories in the region he knew best. His Anglo-Indian critics blamed him because he had not dealt with this and that subject which they thought important. His sympathies lay with the Muslims rather than with the Hindus. He took but a very casual interest in Hinduism and the religion which has so deep-rooted an influence on the great mass of the teeming populations of India. There were qualities in the Muslims that aroused his admiration: he seldom spoke of the Hindus with appreciation. It never seems to have occurred to him that there were among them men of erudition, distinguished scientists and able philosophers. The Bengali, for instance, to him was a coward, a muddler, a braggart, who lost his head in an emergency and shirked responsibility. This is a pity, but it was Kipling's right, as it is of every author, to deal with the subjects that appealed to him.

But I felt that if in this volume I confined myself to Kipling's Indian stories I should not give the reader a fair impression of his varied talent. I have therefore included a few stories with an English setting which have been very widely admired.

It is not to my purpose to give more biographical details of Kipling's life than seem to me useful in my consideration of his short stories. He was born in 1865 at Bombay, where his father was Professor of Architectural Sculpture. When a little more than five his parents took him with his younger sister back to England and placed the two of them in a family where, owing to the unkindness and stupidity of the woman who looked after them, they were miserably unhappy. The wretched little boy was nagged, bullied and beaten. When his mother, after some years, once more came home she was deeply shocked by what she discovered and took the two children away. At the age of twelve Kipling was sent to a school at Westward Ho! It was called the United Services College and had been recently founded to provide education at a small cost for the sons of officers who were to be prepared to go into the army. There were about two hundred boys and they were herded together in a row of lodging-houses. Now, what the school was really like has nothing to do with me; I am only concerned with the picture Kipling has drawn of it in the work of fiction to which he gave the title *Stalky & Co.* A more odious picture of school life can seldom have been drawn. With the exception of the head-master and the chaplain the masters are represented as savage, brutal, narrowminded and incompetent. The boys, supposedly the sons of gentlemen, were devoid of any decent instincts. To the three lads with whom these stories deal Kip-ling gave the names of Stalky, Turkey and Beetle. Stalky was the ringleader. He remained Kipling's ideal of the gallant, resourceful, adventurous, high-spirited soldier and gentle-man. Beetle was Kipling's portrait of himself. The three of them exercised their humour in practical jokes of a singular nastiness. Kipling has narrated them with immense gusto and it is only just to say that the stories are so brilliantly told that though it may give you gooseflesh to read them, when you have once begun you will read them to the end. I should not have dwelt on them at all if it were not plain to me that the influence Kipling was exposed to during the four years he spent at what he called 'the Coll' gained a hold on him which throughout his career he never outgrew. He was never quite able to rid himself of the impressions, the prejudices, the spiritual posture he then acquired. Indeed there is no sign that he wanted to. He retained to the end his relish for the rough and tumble, the ragging, the brutal horseplay of fourth-form schoolboys and their delight in practical jokes. It never seems to have occurred to him that the school was third-rate and the boys a rotten lot. In fact after visiting it many years later he wrote a charming account of it, in which he paid a glowing tribute to that harsh disciplinarian, his old headmaster, and expressed his gratitude for the great benefits he had received during the period he had spent under his care.

When Kipling was a little less than seventeen, his father, who was then curator of the museum at Lahore, got him a job as assistant editor of the English paper, *The Civil and Military Gazette,* which was published in that city, and he left school to return to India. This was in 1882. The world he entered was very different from the world we live in now. Great Britain was at the height of her power. A map showed in pink vast stretches of the earth's surface under the sovereignty of Queen Victoria. The mother country was immensely rich. The British were the world's bankers. British commerce sent its products to the uttermost parts of the earth, and their quality was generally acknowledged to be higher than those manufactured by any other nation. Peace reigned except for small punitive expeditions here and there. The army, though small, was confident (notwithstanding the reverse on Majuba Hill) that it could hold its own against any force that was likely to be brought against it. The British navy was the greatest in the world. In sport the British were supreme. None could compete with them in the games they played, and in the classic races it was almost unheard-of that a horse from abroad should win. It looked as though nothing could ever change this happy state of things. The inhabitants of these islands of ours trusted in God, and God, they were assured, had taken the British Empire under his particular protection. It is true that the Irish were making a nuisance of themselves. It is true that the factory workers were underpaid and overworked. But that seemed an inevitable consequence of the industrialisation of the country and there was nothing to do about it. The reformers who tried to improve their lot were regarded as mischievous troublemakers. It is true that the agricultural labourers lived in miserable hovels and earned a pitiful wage, but the Ladies Bountiful of the landowners were kind to them. Many of them occupied themselves with their moral welfare, sent them beef tea and calves-foot jelly when they were ill and often clothes for their children. People said there always had been rich and poor in the world and always would be, and that seemed to settle the matter.

The British travelled a great deal on the Continent. They crowded the health resorts, Spa, Vichy, Homburg, Aix-les-Bains and Baden-Baden. In winter they went to the Riviera. They built themselves sumptuous villas at Cannes and Monte Carlo. Vast hotels were erected to accommodate them. They had plenty of money and they spent it freely. They felt that they were a race apart and no sooner had they landed at Calais than it was borne in upon them that they were now among natives, not of course natives as were the Indians or the Chinese, but—natives. They alone washed, and the baths that they frequently travelled with were a tangible proof that they were not as others. They were healthy, athletic, sensible, and in every way superior. Because they enjoyed their so-journ among the natives whose habits were so curiously un-English, because, though they thought them frivolous (the French), lazy (the Italians), stupid but funny (the Germans), with the kindness of heart natural to them, they liked them. And they in turn thought that these foreigners liked them. It never entered their heads that the courtesy which they received, the bows, the smiles, the desire to please were owing to their lavish spending, and that behind their backs the 'natives' mocked them for their uncouth dress, their gawkiness, their bad manners, their insolence, their silliness in letting themselves be consistently overcharged, their pa-tronising tolerance; and it required disastrous wars for it to dawn upon them how greatly they had been mistaken. The Anglo-Indian society into which Kipling was introduced when he joined his parents at Lahore shared to the full the prepossessions and the self-complacency of their fellow-subjects in Britain.

Since his short sight prevented him from playing games, Kipling had had the leisure at school to read a great deal and to write. The headmaster seems to have been impressed by the promise he showed and had the good sense to give

him the run of his own library. He wrote the stories which
he afterwards published in book form as *Plain Tales from the
Hills* during such leisure as his duties as sub-editor of *The
Civil and Military Gazette* allowed him. To me their chief
interest is in the picture they give of the society with which
he was dealing. It is a devastating one. There is no sign that
any of the persons he wrote about took any interest in art,
literature or music. The notion seems to have been prevalent
that there was something fishy about a man who took pains
to learn about things Indian. Of one character Kipling wrote:
'he knew as much about Indians as it is good for a man to
know.' A man who was absorbed in his work appears to have
been regarded with misgiving; at best he was eccentric, at
worst a bore. The life described was empty and frivolous.
The self-sufficiency of these people is fearful to contemplate.
And what sort of people were they? They were ordinary
middle-class people, who came from modest homes in England, sons and daughters of retired government servants and
of parsons, doctors and lawyers. The men were empty-
headed; such of them as were in the army or had been to
universities had acquired a certain polish; but the women
were shallow, provincial and genteel. They spent their time
in idle flirtation and their chief amusement seems to have
been to get some man away from another woman. Perhaps
because Kipling wrote in a prudish period which made him
afraid of shocking his readers, perhaps from an innate dis-
inclination to treat of sex, though in these stories there is a
great deal of philandering, it very rarely led to sexual intercourse. Whatever encouragement these women gave the men
whom they attracted, when it came to a showdown they drew
back. They were, in short, what is described in English by
a coarse hyphenated word, and in France, more elegantly,
by *allumeuses*.

It is surprising that Kipling, with his quick mind and
wonderful power of observation, with his wide reading,
should have taken these people at their face value. He was,

of course, very young. *Plain Tales from the Hills* was published when he was only twenty-two. It is perhaps natural
that, coming straight from the brutalities of Westward Ho!
to the unpretentious establishment of the curator of the
Lahore museum, he should have been dazzled on his first
acquaintance with a society that to his inexperienced eyes
had glamour. So was the little bourgeois Marcel dazzled
when he first gained admittance to the exclusive circle of
Madame de Guermantes. Mrs. Hauksbee was neither so brilliant nor so witty as Kipling would have us think. He reveals
her essential drabness when he makes her compare a woman's voice to the grinding brakes of an underground train
coming into Earl's Court station. We are asked to believe
that she was a woman of fashion. If she had been she would
never have gone to Earl's Court except to see an old nurse
and then not by underground, but in a hansom cab.

But *Plain Tales from the Hills* is not only concerned with
Anglo-Indian society. The volume contains stories of Indian
life and stories of the soldiery. When you consider that they
were written when their author was still in his teens or only
just out of them they show an astonishing competence. Kipling said that the best of them were provided for him by his
father. I think we may ascribe this statement to filial piety.
I believe it to be very seldom that an author can make use
of a story given to him ready made, as seldom indeed as a
person in real life can be transferred to fiction just as he is
and maintain an air of verisimilitude. Of course the author
gets his ideas from somewhere, they don't spring out of his
head like Pallas-Athene from the head of her sire in perfect
panoply, ready to be written down. But it is curious how
small a hint, how vague a suggestion, will be enough to give
the author's invention the material to work upon and enable
him in due course to construct a properly disposed story.
Take, for instance, the later story, *The Tomb of his Ancestors*.
It may very well have needed no more than such a casual
remark from one of the officers Kipling had known at Lahore

as: 'Funny chaps these natives are. There was a feller called
So-and-So who was stationed up country among the Bhils,
whose grandfather had kept them in order for donkeys' years
and was buried there, and they got it into their thick heads
that he was a reincarnation of the old man, and he could do
anything he liked with them.' That would have been quite
enough to set Kipling's vivid imagination to work upon what
turned out to be an amusing and delightful tale. *Plain Tales
from the Hills* is very uneven, as indeed Kipling's work always was. That I believe to be inevitable in a writer of short
stories. It is a ticklish thing to write a short story and whether
it is good or bad depends on more than the author's conception, power of expression, skill in construction, invention
and imagination: it depends also on luck. So the clever
Japanese, taking from his little pile of seed pearls, all to his
eyes indistinguishable from one another, the first that comes
to hand and inserting it into the oyster, cannot tell whether
it will turn into a perfect, rounded pearl or a misshapen
object neither of beauty nor of value. Nor is the author a
good judge of his own work. Kipling had a high opinion of
The Phantom 'Rickshaw. I think if he had been more sophisticated when he wrote it, it might have occurred to him
that there was more to be said in extenuation of the man's
behaviour than he apprehended. It is very unfortunate that
you should fall out of love with a married woman with
whom you have had an affair and fall in love with someone
else and want to marry her. But such things happen. And
when the woman won't accept the situation, but pursues you
and waylays you and pesters you with tears and supplica-
tions it is not unnatural that at last you should grow impatient and lose your temper. Mrs. Keith-Wessington is the
most persistent *crampon* in fiction, for even after her death
she continued to harry the wretched man in her phantom
'rickshaw. Jack Pansay deserves our sympathy rather than
our censure. Because a story has been difficult to write an
author may well think better of it than of a story that has

seemed to write itself, sometimes there is a psychological error at the basis of it which he has not noticed, and sometimes he sees in the finished story what he saw in his mind's eye when he conceived it rather than what he has presented to the reader. But we should not be surprised that Kipling sometimes wrote stories which were poor, unconvincing or trivial; we should wonder rather that he wrote so many of such excellence. He was wonderfully various.

In the essay Mr. T. S. Eliot wrote to preface his selection of Kipling's verse he seems to suggest that variety is not a laudable quality in a poet. I would not venture to dispute any opinion of Mr. Eliot's on a question in which poetry is concerned, but though variety may not be a merit in a poet, it surely is in a writer of fiction. The good writer of fiction has the peculiarity, shared to a degree by all men, but in him more abundant, that he has not only one self, but is a queer mixture of several, or, if that seems an extravagant way of putting it, that there are several, often discordant aspects of his personality. The critics could not understand how the same man could write 'Brugglesmith' and Recessional, and so accused him of insincerity. They were unjust. It was the self called Beetle who wrote 'Brugglesmith' and the self called Yardley-Orde who wrote Recessional. When most of us look back on ourselves we can sometimes find consolation in believing that a self in us which we can only deplore has, generally through no merit of ours, perished. The strange thing about Kipling is that the self called Beetle which one would have thought increasing age and the experience of life would have caused to disintegrate, remained alive in all its strength almost to his dying day.

As a child at Bombay Kipling had spoken Hindustani with his ayah and the servants as his native language and in *Something of Myself* he has told that when he was taken to see his parents he translated what he had to say into broken English. It may be supposed that on his return to India he quickly recovered his old knowledge of the language. In the same book he has related in terms that couldn't be bettered how at Lahore he got the material which so soon afterwards he was to make effective use of. As a reporter 'I described openings of big bridges and such-like, which meant a night to two with the engineers; floods on railways—more nights in the wet with wretched heads of repair gangs; village festivals and consequent oubreaks of cholera or smallpox; communal riots under the shadow of the Mosque of Wazir Khan, where the patient waiting troops lay in timber-yards or side-alleys till the order came to go in and hit the crowds on the feet with the gunbutt, and the growling, flaring, creed-drunk city would be brought to hand without effusion of blood' . . . Often at night 'I would wander till dawn in all manner of odd places—liquor-shops, gambling- and opium-dens, which are not a bit mysterious, wayside entertainments such as puppet-shows, native dances; or in and about the narrow gullies under the Mosque of Wazir Khan for the sheer sake of looking . . . And there were "wet" nights too at the Club or one Mess, when a tableful of boys, half crazed with discomfort, but with just sense enough to stick to beer and bones which seldom betray, tried to rejoice and somehow succeeded . . . I got to meet the soldiery of those days in visits to Fort Lahore and, in a less degree, at Mian Mir Cantonments. . . . Having no position to consider, and my trade enforcing it, I could move at will in the fourth dimension. I came to realize the bare horrors of the private's life, and the unnecessary torments he endured on account of the Christian doctrine that lays it down that "the wages of sin is death."'

I have included in this selection two stories in which figure the three privates, Mulvaney, Learoyd and Ortheris. They have been immensely popular. I think they have the disadvantage for most readers that they are written in the peculiar dialect of the speakers. It is no easy matter to decide how far an author should go in this direction. Manifestly it would be absurd to make men like Mulvaney and Ortheris deliver themselves in the cultured language of a don at King's, but to make them speak consistently in dialect may well make a narrative tedious. Perhaps the best plan is to use the turns of phrase, the grammar and the vocabulary of the persons concerned, but to reproduce peculiarities of pronunciation so sparingly as not to incommode the reader. That was not, however, Kipling's way. He reproduced the accents of his three soldiers phonetically. No one has found fault with Learoyd's Yorkshire, which was corrected by Kipling's father, himself a Yorkshireman; but critics have claimed that neither Mulvaney's Irish nor Ortheris's cockney was real. Kipling was a master of description and could relate incident brilliantly, but it does not seem to me that his dialogue was always plausible. He put into the mouth of Ortheris expressions he could never have used and one may well ask oneself how on earth he came by a quotation from Macaulay's *Lays of Ancient Rome*. I cannot believe that a well-bred woman such as the Brushwood Boy's mother is supposed to be would speak to him of his father as 'the pater.' Sometimes the language used by the officers and officials in Indian is unconvincingly hearty. To my mind Kipling's dialogue is only beyond reproach when he is translating into measured, dignified English the speech of Indians. The reader will remember that as a child talking with his parents he had to translate what he had to say from Hindustani into English: it may be that that was the form of speech that came most naturally to him.

In 1887 Kipling, after five years as sub-editor of *The Civil and Military Gazette,* was sent to Allahabad, several hundred miles to the south, to work on the much more important sister-paper, *The Pioneer*. The proprietors were starting a weekly edition for home, and he was given the editorship. An entire page was devoted to fiction. The *Plain Tales from the Hills* had been restricted to twelve hundred words, but now he was allotted sufficient space to write stories up to five thousand. He wrote 'soldier tales, Indian tales, and tales of the opposite sex.' Among them were such powerful but gruesome stories as *The Mark of the Beast* and *The Return of Imray.*

The stories Kipling wrote during this period were published in six paper-covered volumes in Wheeler's Indian Railway Library, and with the money he thus earned and a commission to write travel sketches he left India for England 'by way of the Far East and the United States.' This was in 1889. He had spent seven years in India. His stories had become known in England and when he arrived in London, still a very young man, he found editors eager to accept whatever he wrote. He settled down in Villiers Street, Strand. The stories he produced there are of the highest quality, a quality which later he often achieved but never surpassed. Among them are *On Greenhow Hill, The Courting of Dinah Shadd, The Man Who Was, Without Benefit of Clergy* and *At the End of the Passage.* It looks as though the new surroundings in which he found himself brought into greater vividness his recollections of India. That is a likely enough thing to happen. When an author is living in the scene of his story, perhaps among the people who have suggested the characters of his invention, he may well find himself bewildered by the mass of his impressions. He cannot see the wood for the trees. But absence will erase from his memory redundant details and inessential facts. He will get then a bird's-eye view, as it were, of his subject and so, with less material to embarrass him, can get the form into his story which completes it.

It was then too that he wrote the tale which he called 'The Finest Story in the World.' It is interesting because he dealt in it, for the first time, I think, with metempsychosis. It was natural that the theme should interest him, for the belief in it is ingrained in the Hindu sensibility. It is as little a matter of doubt to the people of India as were the Virgin Birth of Christ and the Resurrection to the Christians of the thirteenth century. No one can have travelled in India without discovering how deep-rooted the belief is not only among the uneducated, but among men of culture and of experience in world affairs. One hears in conversation, or reads in the papers, of men who claim to remember something of their past lives. In this story Kipling has dealt with it with great imaginative power. He returned to it in a story which is less well-known called 'Wireless.' In this he made effective use of what was then a new toy for the scientifically minded amateur to persuade the reader of the possibility that the chemist's assistant of his tale, dying of tuberculosis, might under the effect of a drug recall that past life of his in which he was John Keats. To anyone who has stood in the little room in Rome overlooking the steps that lead down to the Piazza di Spagna and seen the drawing Joseph Severn made of the emaciated, beautiful head of the dead poet, Kipling's story is wonderfully pathetic. It is thrilling to watch the dying chemist's assistant, in love too, worrying out in a trance-like state, lines that Keats wrote in The Eve of St. Agnes. It is a lovely story admirably told.

Six years later Kipling, in the entrancing tale The Tomb of his Ancestors, to which I have already referred, took up once more the theme of metempsychosis, and this time in such a way as not to outrage probability. It is the Bhils, the mountain tribes among whom the story is set, who believe that the young subaltern, its hero, is a reincarnation of his grandfather who spent many years in their midst and whose memory they still revere. Kipling never succeeded better in creating that indefinable quality which for want of a better word we call atmosphere.

After spending two years in London, years of hard work, Kipling's health broke down, and he very sensibly decided to take the rest of a long journey. He returned to England to be married and with his bride started off on a tour of the world, but financial difficulties obliged him to cut it short, and he settled down in Vermont where his wife's family had long been established. This was in the summer of 1892. He stayed there off and on till 1896. During those four years he wrote a number of stories many of which were of a quality which only he could reach. It was then that he wrote *In the Rukh* in which Mowgli makes his first appearance. It was a propitious inspiration, for from it sprang the two *Jungle Books* in which, to my mind, his great and varied gifts found their most brilliant expression. They show his wonderful talent for telling a story, they have a delicate humour and they are romantic and plausible. The device of making animals talk is as old as Aesop's fables, and for all I know much older, and La Fontaine, as we know, employed it with charm and wit, but I think no one has performed the difficult feat of persuading the reader that it is as natural for animals to speak as for human beings more triumphantly than Kipling has done in *The Jungle Books*. He had used the same device in the story called *A Walking Delegate* in which horses indulge in political discussion, but there is in the story an obviously didactic element which prevents it from being successful.

It was during these fertile years that Kipling wrote *The Brushwood Boy,* a story which has deeply impressed so many people that, though it is not one of my favourites, I have thought it well to print it in this selection. He availed himself in this of a notion which has attracted writers of fiction both before and after him, the notion, namely, of two persons systematically dreaming the same dreams. The difficulty of it lies in making the dreams interesting. We listen restlessly when someone at the breakfast table insists on telling us of the dream he had during the night, and a dream described on paper is apt to arouse in us the same impatience. Kipling had before done the same sort of thing, though on a smaller scale, in *The Bridge-Builders*. There I think he made a mistake. He had a good story to tell. It is about a flood that suddenly rushes down on a bridge over the Ganges which, after three years of strenuous labour, is on the point of completion. There is doubt in the minds of the two white men in charge of the operations whether three of the spans, still unfinished, will stand the strain, and they fear that if the stone-boats go adrift the girders will be damaged. They have received by telegram warning that the flood is on the way, and with their army of workmen spend an agonized night doing what they can to strengthen the weak places. All this is described with force and the telling detail of which Kipling was a master. The bridge stands the strain and all is well. That is all. It may be that Kipling thought it wasn't enough. Findlayson, the chief engineer, has been too anxious and too fully occupied to bother about eating anything and by the second night is all in. His lascar aide persuades him to swallow some opium pills. Then news comes that a wire hawser has snapped and the stone-boats are loose. Findlayson and the lascar rush down to the bank and get into one of the stone-boats in the hope of preventing them from doing irreparable injury. The pair are swept down the river and landed half-drowned on an island. Exhausted and doped they fall asleep and dream the same dream in which they see the Hindu Gods in animal form, Ganesh the elephant, Hanuman the ape and finally Krishna himself, and hear them talk. When the two wake in the morning they are rescued. But the double dream is needless and because the conversation of the Gods is needless too it is tedious.

In *The Brushwood Boy* the identical dreams are an essential element in the story. It is here for the reader to read and I hope he will agree with me that Kipling has described these dreams with felicity. They are strange, romantic, frightening and mysterious. The long series of dreams which these two people have shared from their childhood seems, though you don't quite know why, so significant of something of high import that it is somewhat of a disappointment that such amazing occurrences should result in no more than 'boy meets girl.' It is of course the same difficulty that confronts the reader of the first part of Goethe's *Faust*. It seems hardly worth while for Faust to have bartered his soul to see Mephistopheles do conjuring tricks in a wine-cellar and to effect the seduction of a lowly maid. I find it difficult to look upon *The Brushwood Boy* as one of Kipling's best stories. The persons concerned in it are really too good to be true. The Brushwood Boy is heir to a fine estate. He is idolized by his parents, by the keeper who taught him to shoot, by the servants, by the tenants. He is a good shot, a good rider, a hard worker, a brave soldier adored by his men, and after a battle on the North-West Frontier is awarded a D.S.O. and becomes the youngest major in the British army. He is clever, sober and chaste. He is perfect and incredible. But though I carp I cannot deny that it remains a good and moving story admirably told. One must look upon it not as a tale that has any relation to real life, but as much of a fairy story as *The Sleeping Beauty* or *Cinderella*.

It was on his short periods of leave that Kipling came to know that Anglo-Indian society which he wrote about in *Plain Tales from the Hills,* but his experiences as a reporter, so well set forth in the passage I quoted earlier in this essay, surely made it plain to him that in those little stories he had described but one aspect of Anglo-Indian life. What he saw on his various assignments deeply impressed him. I have already spoken of *The Bridge-Builders* with its fine account of those men who on little pay, with small chance of recognition, gave their youth, their strength, their health to do to the best of their ability the job it was their business to do. In the unfortunately named *William the Conqueror* Kipling has written a tale in which he shows how two or three ordinary, rather commonplace men, and a woman, the William of the story, fought a disastrous famine all through the hot weather and saved a horde of children from dying of starvation. It is a tale of selfless, stubborn tenacity soberly narrated. In these two stories and in several more, Kipling has told of the obscure men and women who devoted their lives to the service of India. They made many mistakes, for they were but human. Many were stupid. Many were hidebound with prejudice. Many were unimaginative. They kept the peace.

They administered justice. They built the roads, the bridges, the railways. They fought famine, flood and pestilence. They treated the sick. It remains to be seen whether those who have succeeded them, not in high place, but in those modest situations in the hands of whose occupants the lot of the common man depends will make as good a job of it as they did.

William the Conqueror is not only the story of a famine; it is a love story as well. I have mentioned the fact that Kipling seems to have shied away, like an unbroken colt, from any treatment of sex. In the Mulvaney stories he makes casual reference to the amours of the soldiery and in *Something of Myself* he has an indignant passage in which he remarks on the stupid and criminal folly of the authorities who counted it impious 'that bazaar prostitutes should be inspected; or that the men should be taught elementary precautions in their dealings with them. This official virtue cost our army in India nine thousand expensive white men a year always laid up from venereal disease.' But he is concerned then not with love, but with an instinct of normal man that demands its satisfaction. I can only remember two stories in which Kipling has attempted (successfully) to represent passion. One is *'Love-o'-Women,'* which for this reason I have inserted in this book. It is a terrible, perhaps brutal story, but it is finely and vigorously told, and the end, mysterious and left unexplained though it be, is powerful. Critics have found fault with this end. Matisse once showed a picture of his to a visitor who exclaimed: 'I've never seen a woman like that', to which he replied: 'It isn't a woman, madam, it's a picture.' If the painter is permitted certain distortions to achieve the effect he is aiming at, there can be no reason why the writer of fiction should not accord himself the same freedom. Probability is not something settled once for all; it is what you can get your readers to accept as such. Kipling was not writing an official report, he was writing a story. It was his right to make it dramatically effective, if that is what he wanted to do, and if the gentleman-ranker of the story might not have said in real life to the woman he had seduced and ruined the words Kipling has put into his mouth, that is no matter. It is plausible and the reader is moved as Kipling intended him to be.

The other story in which Kipling has depicted genuine passion is *Without Benefit of Clergy*. It is a beautiful and pathetic tale. If I had to choose for an anthology the best story Kipling ever wrote, this I believe is the one I would choose. Other stories are more characteristic, *The Head of the District*, for instance, but in this one he has come as near as the medium allows to what the story-teller aims at, but can hardly hope to achieve—perfection.

I have been led to write the above on account of the love scene which gives *William the Conqueror* its happy ending. It is strangely embarrassing. The two persons concerned are in love with one another; that is made clear; but there is nothing of ecstasy in their love, it is a rather humdrum affair, with already a kind of domestic quality about it. They are two very nice sensible people who will make a good job of married life. The love scene is adolescent. You would expect a schoolboy home for the holidays to talk like that with the local doctor's young daughter, not two grown, efficient persons who have just gone through a harrowing and dangerous experience.

As a rough generalization I would suggest that an author reaches the height of his powers when he is between thirty-five and forty. It takes him till then to learn what Kipling made a point of calling his trade. Till then his work is immature, tentative and experimental. By profiting by past mistakes, by the mere process of living, which brings him experience and a knowledge of human nature, by discovering his own limitations and learning what subjects he is competent to deal with and how best to deal with them, he acquires command over his medium. He is in possession of such talent as he has. He will produce the best work he is capable of for perhaps fifteen years, for twenty if he is lucky, and then his powers gradually dwindle. He loses the vigour of imagination which he had in his prime. He has given all he had to give. He will go on writing, for writing is a habit easy to contract, but hard to break, but what he writes will be only an increasingly pale reminder of what he wrote at his prime.

It was different with Kipling. He was immensely precocious. He was in full possession of his powers almost from the very beginning. Some of the stories in *Plain Tales from the Hills* are so trivial that later in life he would probably not have thought them worth writing, but they are told clearly, vividly and effectively. Technically there is no fault to find with them. Such faults as they have are owing to the callowness of his youth and not to his want of skill. And when, only just out of his teens, he was transferred to Allahabad and was able to express himself at greater length he wrote a series of tales which can justly be described as masterly. On his first arrival in London, the editor of *Macmillan's Magazine*, whom he had gone to see, asked him how old he was. It is no wonder that when Kipling told him that in a few months he would be twenty-four, he cried 'My God!' His accomplishment by then was truly amazing.

But all things have to be paid for in this world. By the end of the century, that is by the time Kipling was thirty-five, he had written his best stories. I do not mean that after that he wrote bad stories, he couldn't have done that if he'd tried, they were well enough in their way, but they lacked the magic with which the early Indian stories had been infused. It was only when, returning in fancy to the scene of his early life in India, he wrote *Kim*, that he regained it. *Kim* is his masterpiece. It must seem strange at first that Kipling after leaving Allahabad never went back to India except for a short visit to his parents at Lahore. After all it was his Indian stories that had brought him his immense fame. He himself called it notoriety, but it was fame. I can only suppose that he felt India had given him all the subjects he could deal with. Once, after he had spent a period in the West Indies he sent me a message to say that I should do well to go there, for there were plenty of stories to be written about the people of the islands, but they were not the sort of stories he could write. He must have felt that there were plenty of stories in India besides those he had written, but that they too were not the sort of stories he could write. For him the vein was worked out.

The Boer War came to pass and Kipling went to South Africa. In India he had conceived a boyish, touching if rather absurd admiration for the officers with whom he was brought in contact. But these gallant gentlemen who cut so fine a figure on the polo field, at gymkhanas, dances and picnics, showed a horrifying incapacity when it came to waging a war very different from the punitive expeditions they had conducted on the North-West Frontier. Officers and men were as brave as he had always thought them, but they were ill led. He surveyed the muddle of that unhappy war with consternation. Did he see that this was the first rent in that great fabric, the British Empire, which was his pride and to the awareness of which he had done so much, in verse and prose, to awaken his fellow-subjects? He wrote two stories, *The Captive* and *The Way that He Took*, in which he attacked the inefficiency of the authorities at home and the incompetence of the officers in command. They are good stories, and if I have not given them a place in this volume it is because of the strong element of propaganda in them and because like all stories that have a topical interest the passage of time has deprived them of significance.

I should warn the reader that my opinion that Kipling's best stories are those of which the scene is laid in India is by no means shared by eminent critics. They think those Kipling wrote in what they call his third period show a depth, an insight and a compassion of which they deplore the lack in his Indian tales. For them the height of his achievement is to be found in such stories as *An Habitation Enforced, A Madonna of the Trenches, The Wish House* and *Friendly Brook. An Habitation Enforced* is a charming story, but surely rather obvious; and though the other three are good enough they do not seem to me remarkable. It did not need an author of Kipling's great gifts to write them. *Just So Stories, Puck of Pook's Hill* and *Rewards and Fairies* are children's books and their worth must be judged by the pleasure they afforded children. This *Just So Stories* must have done. One can almost hear the squeals of laughter with which they listened to the story of how the elephant got his trunk. In the two other books Puck appears to a little boy and a little girl and produces for their instruction various characters by means of whom they may gain an elementary and romantic acquaintance with English history. I don't think this was a happy device. The stories are of course well contrived; I like best *On the Great Wall,* in which Parnesius, the Roman legionary, appears, but I should have liked it better if it had been a straightforward reconstruction of an episode in the Roman occupation of Britain.

The only story Kipling wrote after he settled down in England that I would on no account leave out of this selection is *'They.'* (In reading it you must keep in mind that his use of the House Beautiful for the country house in which the events he relates take place, reminding one of Ye Olde Tea-Shoppe and horrors of the same sort, had not been made obnoxious by the vulgar purveyors of whimsy and the pretty-pretty.) *'They'* is a fine and deeply moving effort of the imagination. In 1899 Kipling went with his wife and children to New York, and he and his elder daughter caught colds which turned into pneumonia. Those of us who are old enough can remember the world-wide concern when the cables told us that Kipling lay at death's door. He recovered, but his daughter died. It cannot be doubted that *'They'* was inspired by his enduring grief at her loss. Heine said: 'Out of my great griefs I make these little songs.' Kipling wrote an exquisite story. Some people have found it obscure and others sentimental. One of the hazards that confront the writer of fiction is the danger of slipping from sentiment into sentimentality. The distinction between the two is fine. It may be that sentimentality is merely sentiment that you don't happen to like. Kipling had the gift of drawing tears, but sometimes, in his stories not for children, but about children, they are tears you resent, for the emotion that draws them is mawkish. There is nothing obscure in 'They' and to my mind nothing sentimental.

Kipling was deeply interested in the invention and discoveries which were then transforming our civilization. The reader will remember what effective use he made of wireless in the story of that name. He was fascinated by machines and when he was fascinated by a subject he wrote stories about it. He took a great deal of trouble to get his facts right, and if sometimes he made mistakes, as all authors do, the facts were so unfamiliar to most readers that they did not know. He indulged in technical details for their own sake, not to show off, since though argumentative and self-opinionated as a man, he was modest and unassuming as an author, but for the fun of it. He was like a concert pianist rejoicing in the brilliant ease of his execution who chooses a piece not because of its musical value, but because it gives him an opportunity to exercise his special gift. In one of his stories Kipling says that he had to interrupt the narrator over and over again to ask him to explain his technical terms. The reader of these stories, and he wrote a number of them, unable to do this, remains perplexed. They would be more readable if their author had been less meticulous. In 'Their Lawful Occasions,' for instance, I surmise that only a naval officer could fully understand what goes on, and I am quite prepared to believe that *he* would find it a jolly good yarn. .007 is a story about a locomotive, *The Ship that Found Herself*, a story about an ocean tramp; I think you would have to be respectively an engine-driver and a ship-builder to read them with comprehension. In *The Jungle Books*, and indeed in *The Maltese Cat*, Kipling made the various animals concerned talk in a highly convincing manner; he used the same device in the locomotive numbered .007 and in the ship named *Dimbula*. I do not think with advantage. I cannot believe that the ordinary reader knows (or cares) what a garboard strake is, or a bilge-stringer, a high-pressure cylinder or a web-frame.

These stories show another side of Kipling's varied talent, but I have not thought it necessary to include any of them in this selection. The object of fiction (from the reader's standpoint from which the author's may often be very different) is entertainment; and as such to my mind their value is small.

I have been more doubtful about those stories concerned with practical joking, ragging, and drunkenness which he wrote from time to time. There was a Rabelaisian streak in him which the hypocrisy of the times, with its deliberate turning away from what are known as the facts of life, constrained him to express in the description of horseplay and inebriation. In *Something of Myself* he tells how he showed a story about the 'opposite sex' to his mother, who 'abolished it' and wrote to him: 'Never you do that again.' From the context one may conclude that it dealt with adultery. Whether you find drunkenness amusing depends, I suppose, on your personal idiosyncrasies. It has been my ill-fortune to live much among drunkards, and for my part I have found them boring at their best and disgusting at their worst. But it is evident that this feeling of mine is rare. That stories dealing with drunkards have a strong allure is shown by the popularity of Brugglesmith, a crapulous ruffian, and of Pyecroft, a sottish petty officer, who amused Kipling so much that he wrote several tales about him. Practical joking, till the very recent past, seems to have had an appeal that was universal. Spanish literature of the Golden Age is full of it and everyone remembers the cruel practical jokes that were played on Don Quixote. In the Victorian Age it was still thought funny and from a recently published book we may learn that it was practised with delight in the highest circles. Here again it depends on your temperament whether it amuses you or whether it doesn't. I must confess that I read Kipling's stories which deal with this subject with discomfort. And the hilarity which overcomes the perpetrators of the exploit grates upon me; they are not content with laughing at the humiliation of their victim; they lean against one another helpless with laughter, they roll off their chairs, they collapse shrieking, they claw the carpet; and in one story the narrator takes a room at an inn so that he may have his laugh out. There is only one of these tales that I have found frankly amusing and since I thought it only right to give the reader at least one example of this kind of story I have printed it in this volume. It is called *The Village that Voted the Earth Was Flat*. Here the comedy is rich, the victim deserves his punishment, and his punishment is severe without being brutal.

I have in this essay only referred casually to Kipling's success. It was enormous. Nothing like it had been seen since Dickens took the reading world by storm with *The Pickwick Papers*. Nor did he have to wait for it. Already in 1890 Henry James was writing to Stevenson that Kipling, 'the star of the hour,' was Stevenson's nearest rival and Stevenson was writing to Henry James that Kipling was 'too clever to live.' It looks as though they were both a trifle taken aback by the appearance of this 'infant monster' as James called him. They acknowledged his brilliant parts, but with reservations. 'He amazes me by his precocity and various endowment,' wrote Stevenson. 'But he alarms me by his copiousness and haste. . . . I was never capable of—and surely never guilty of—such a debauch of production . . . I look on, I admire, I rejoice for myself; but in a kind of ambition we all have for our tongue and literature I am wounded. . . . Certainly Kipling has gifts; the fairy godmothers were all tipsy at his christening: what will he do with them?'

But copiousness is not a defect in a writer; it is a merit. All the greatest authors have had it. Of course not all their production is of value; only the mediocre can sustain a constant level. It is because the great authors wrote a great deal that now and then they produced great works. Kipling was no exception. I don't believe any writer is a good judge of the writing of his contemporaries, for he naturally likes best the sort of thing he does himself. It is difficult for him to appreciate merits that he does not possess. Stevenson and James were not ungenerous men and they recognized Kipling's great abilities, but from what we know of them we can guess how disconcerted they were by the boisterous exuberance and the sentimentality of some of his tales and the brutality and grimness of others.

Of course Kipling had his detractors. The plodding writers who after years of labour had achieved but a modest place in the literary world found it hard to bear that this young man, coming from nowhere, without any of the social graces, should win, apparently with little effort, so spectacular a success; and as we know, they consoled themselves by prophesying (as once before they had of Dickens) that as he had come up like a rocket he would go down like the stick. It was objected to Kipling that he put too much of himself into his stories. But when you come down to brass tacks what else has an author to give you but himself? Sometimes, like Sterne for instance, or Charles Lamb, he gives you himself with a beguiling frankness, it is both the inspiration and the mainstay of his creativity; but even though he tries his best to be objective what he writes is inevitably infused with his ego. You cannot read a dozen pages of *Madame Bovary* without receiving a strong impression of Flaubert's irascible, pessimistic, morbid and self-centred personality. Kipling's critics were wrong to blame him for introducing his personality into his stories. What they meant of course was that they did not like the personality he presented to them; and that is understandable. In his early work he exhibited characteristics which were offensive. You received the impression of a bumptious, arrogant young man, extravagantly cock-sure and knowing; and this necessarily excited the antagonism of his critics. For such an assumption of superiority as these rather unamiable traits indicate affronts one's self-esteem.

Kipling was widely accused of vulgarity: so were Balzac and Dickens; I think only because they dealt with aspects of life that offended persons of refinement. We are tougher now: when we call someone refined we do not think we are paying him a compliment. But one of the most absurd charges brought against him was that his stories were anecdotes, which the critics who made it thought was to condemn him (as they sometimes still do); but if they had troubled to consult the Oxford Dictionary they would have seen that a meaning it gives to the word is: 'The narration of a detached incident, or of a single event, told as being in itself interesting or striking.' That is a perfect definition of a short story. The story of Ruth, the story of the Matron of Ephesus, Boccaccio's story of Federigo degli Alberighi and his falcon are all anecdotes. So are *Boule de Suif*, *La Parure and L'Héritage*. An anecdote is the bony structure of a story which gives it form and coherence and which the author clothes with flesh, blood and nerves. No one is obliged to read stories, and if you don't like them unless there is something in them more than a story, there is nothing to do about it. You may not like oysters, no one can blame you for that, but it is unreasonable to condemn them because they don't possess the emotional quality of a beefsteak and kidney pudding. It is equally unreasonable to find fault with a story because it is only a story. That is just what some of Kipling's detractors have done. He was a very talented man, but not a profound thinker—indeed I cannot think of any great novelist who was; he had a consummate gift for telling a certain kind of story and he enjoyed telling it. He was wise enough for the most part to do what he could do best. As he was a sensible man, he was no doubt pleased when people liked his stories and took it with a shrug of the shoulders when they didn't.

Another fault found with him was that he had little power of characterization. I don't think the critics who did this quite understood the place of characterization in a short story. Of course you can write a story with the intention of displaying a character. Flaubert did it in *Un Coeur Simple* and Chekhov in *The Darling*, which Tolstoi thought so well of; though a purist might object that they are not short stories, but potted novels. Kipling was concerned with incident. In a tale so concerned you need only tell enough about the persons who take part in it to bring them to life; you show them at the moment you are occupied with; they are inevitably static. To show the development of character an author needs the passage of time and the elbow-room of a novel. Perhaps the most remarkable character in fiction is Julien Sorel, but how could Stendhal have shown the development of his complicated character in a short story? Now, I suggest that Kipling drew his characters quite firmly enough for his purpose. There is a distinction to be made between 'characters' and character. Mulvaney, Ortheris and Learoyd are 'characters.' It is easy enough to create them. Findlayson in *The Bridge-Builders,* and Scott and William in *William the Conqueror* have character; and to delineate that is much more difficult. It is true that they are very ordinary, commonplace people, but that gives point to the narrative, and surely Kipling was well aware of it. The father and mother of the Brushwood Boy are not, as Kipling thought, 'County,' landed gentry living on an ancestral estate, but a nice, worthy couple from Arnold Bennett's *Five Towns* who, after amassing a competence, had settled down in the country. Though lightly sketched, they are alive, recognizable human beings. Mrs. Hauksbee was not the fashionable and distinguished creature he thought her, she was a rather second-rate little woman with a very good opinion of herself, but she is far from a lay-figure. We have all met her. Yardley-Orde in *The Head of the District* dies four pages after the story opens, but so sufficiently has Kipling characterized him that anyone could write his life-history, after the pattern of one of Aubrey's *Lives*, with a very fair chance that it would be accurate. I hurry on so that I may not yield to the temptation of writing it here and now to show how easily it could be done.

A distinguished author not long ago told me that he disliked Kipling's style so much that he could not read him. The critics of his own day seem to have found it abrupt, jerky and mannered. One of them said that 'it must be insisted that slang is not strength, nor does the abuse of the full stop ensure crispness.' True. An author uses slang to reproduce conversation accurately and in the course of his narrative to give his prose a conversational air. The chief objection to it is that its vogue is transitory and in a few years it is dated and may even be incomprehensible. Sometimes of course it passes into the language and then gains a literary validity so that not even a purist can object to its use. Kipling wrote in shorter sentences than were at that time usual. That can no longer surprise us, and since the lexicographers tell us that a sentence is a series of words, forming the grammatically complete expression of a single thought, there seems no reason why, when an author has done just this, he should not point the fact with a full stop. He is indeed right to do so. George Moore, no lenient critic of his contemporaries, admired Kipling's style for its sonority and its rhythm. 'Others have written more beautifully, but no one that I can call to mind has written so copiously. . . . He writes with the whole language, with the language of the Bible, and with the language of the street.' Kipling's vocabulary was rich. He chose his words, often very unexpected words, for their colour, their precision, their cadence. He knew what he wanted to say and said it incisively. His prose, with which alone I am concerned, had pace and vigour. Like every other author he had his mannerisms. Some, like his unseemly addiction to biblical phrases, he quickly discarded; others he retained. He continued throughout his life to begin a sentence with a relative. Which was a pity. He continued to make deplorable use of the poetic *ere* when it would have been more natural to say *before*. Once at least he wrote *e'en* for *even*. These are minor points. Kipling has so made his style his own that I don't suppose anyone to-day would care to write like him, even if he could, but I don't see how one can deny that the instrument he constructed was admirably suited to the purpose to which he put it. He seldom indulged in long descriptions, but with his seeing eye and quick perception he was able by means of this instrument to put before the reader with extreme vividness the crowded Indian scene in all its fantastic variety.

If in this essay I have not hesitated to point out what seemed to me Kipling's defects, I hope I have made it plain how great I think were his merits. The short story is not a form of fiction in which the English have on the whole excelled. The English, as their novels show, are inclined to diffuseness. They have never been much interested in form. Succinctness goes against their grain. But the short story demands form. It demands succinctness. Diffuseness kills it. It depends on construction. It does not admit of loose ends. It must be complete in itself. All these qualities you will find in Kipling's stories when he was at his magnificent best, and this, happily for us, he was in story after story. Rudyard Kipling is the only writer of short stories our country has produced who can stand comparison with Guy de Maupassant and Chekhov. He is our greatest story writer. I can't believe he will ever be equalled. I am sure he can never be excelled.

Traveller's Library

ESSAYS

Swinburne – Edmund Gosse
Robert Louis Stevenson – Edmund Gosse
No. 2 The Pines – Max Beerbohm
Wordsworth in the Tropics – Aldous Huxley
Reminiscences of Conrad – John Galsworthy
A Hermit's Day – Desmond MacCarthy
Dr. Burney's Evening Party – Virginia Woolf
How to Know a Good Book from a Bad – H. W. Garrod
Florence Nightingale – Lytton Strachey
Religion and Science: Old Wine in New Bottles –
    Julian Huxley
The Last Judgment – J. B. S. Haldane
On the Value of Scepticism – Bertrand Russell
Eastern and Western Ideals of Happiness – Bertrand Russell
A Free Man's Worship – Bertrand Russell
A Night at Pietramala – Aldous Huxley

SHORT STORIES

Mrs. Johnson – Norah Hoult
The Machine Breaks Down – Osbert Sitwell
The Man with the Broken Nose – Michael Arlen
Biography – Martin Armstrong
The Poet and the Mandrill – Martin Armstrong
The Big Drum – William Gerhardi
Pictures – Katherine Mansfield
Psychology – Katherine Mansfield
Miss Brill – Katherine Mansfield
The Marquis de Chaumont – Harold Nicolson
Arketall – Harold Nicolson
Lady into Fox – David Garnett
Louise – Saki (H. H. Munro)
Tobermory – Saki (H. H. Munro)
Esmé – Saki (H. H. Munro)

POEMS

The Making of a Poet – Roy Campbell
The Serf – Roy Campbell
Horses on Camargue – Roy Campbell
On Some South African Novelists – Roy Campbell
"Blighters" – Siegfried Sassoon
Base Details – Siegfried Sassoon
Idyll – Siegfried Sassoon
Vision – Siegfried Sassoon
Everyone Sang – Siegfried Sassoon
Tarantella – Hilaire Belloc
Lines to a Don – Hilaire Belloc
The Statue – Hilaire Belloc
On a Dead Hostess – Hilaire Belloc
On a Great Election – Hilaire Belloc
Partly from the Greek – Hilaire Belloc
Autumn Evening – Frances Cornford
To a Lady Seen from the Train – Frances Cornford
In the Caves of Auvergne – W. J. Turner
The Bull – Ralph Hodgson
The Mystery – Ralph Hodgson
Leisure – William H. Davies
Sea-Fever – John Masefield
I See His Blood upon the Rose – Joseph Plunkett
The Rio Grande – Sacheverell Sitwell
A Passer-By – Robert Bridges
On a Dead Child – Robert Bridges
Nightingales – Robert Bridges
Renouncement – Alice Meynell
The Hound of Heaven – Francis Thompson
The Kingdom of God (In No Strange Land) –
    Francis Thompson
The Soldier – Rupert Brooke
The Hill – Rupert Brooke
The Old Vicarage, Grantchester – Rupert Brooke
Heaven – Rupert Brooke
An Epitaph – Walter de la Mare
The Three Strangers – Walter de la Mare
The Little Salamander – Walter de la Mare
Arabia – Walter de la Mare
The Listeners – Walter de la Mare

The Golden Journey to Samarkand: Prologue –
  James Elroy Flecker
War Song of the Saracens – James Elroy Flecker
The Old Ships – James Elroy Flecker
Brumana – James Elroy Flecker
Hyali – James Elroy Flecker
Down by the Salley Gardens – William Butler Yeats
The Lake Isle of Innisfree – William Butler Yeats
When You Are Old – William Butler Yeats
To a Friend Whose Work Has Come to Nothing –
  William Butler Yeats
That the Night Come – William Butler Yeats

NOVELS

The Old Wives' Tale – Arnold Bennett
Trent's Last Case – E. C. Bentley

Tellers of Tales

Tobermory – Saki
To Build a Fire – Jack London
The Death of Iván Ilých – Leo Tolstoy
The Toupee Artist – Nicolai Lyeskov
Mouzhiks – Anton Chekhov
Twenty-Six and One – Maxim Gorky
Sunstroke – Ivan Bunin
Captain Ribnikov – Alexander Kuprin
Hydromel – Vassili Iretsky
Without Cherry Blossom – Pantaleimon Romanof
In the Town of Berdichev – Vassili Grossman
Hunger – Alexander Neweroff
Romance – Vera Inber
Earth on the Hands – Boris Pilnjak
A Letter – Isaac Babel
The Child – Vsevolod Ivanov
The Customer – Georgy Peskov
The Knives – Valentine Katayev
Pippo Spano – Heinrich Mann
Old Rogaum and His Theresa – Theodore Dreiser
A. V. Laider – Max Beerbohm
The Amulet – Jacob Wassermann
Cavalry Patrol – Hugo von Hofmannsthal
Seeds – Sherwood Anderson
The Other Woman – Sherwood Anderson
Early Sorrow – Thomas Mann
Mr. and Mrs. Abbey's Difficulties – E. M. Forster
The Invisible Collection – Stefan Zweig
Uncle Fred Flits By – P. G. Wodehouse
In the Last Coach – Leonhard Frank
Counterparts – James Joyce
The Tragedy of Goupil – Louis Pergaud
Odour of Chrysanthemums – D. H. Lawrence
The Chink – Alexander Arnoux
Haircut – Ring Lardner
Champion – Ring Lardner
A Balaam – Arnold Zweig
Old Man Minick – Edna Ferber
The Golden Beetle – Bruno Frank
The Catalan Night – Paul Morand
Silent Snow, Secret Snow – Conrad Aiken
The Lovely Day – Jacques de Lacretelle

On the Farm – Hans Friedrich Blunck
The Killers – Ernest Hemingway
The Stranger – Katherine Mansfield
The House of Mourning – Franz Werfel
A Start in Life – Ruth Suckow
The Desert Islander – Stella Benson
Big Blonde – Dorothy Parker
Orphant Annie – Thyra Samter Winslow
Nuns at Luncheon – Aldous Huxley
The Rich Boy – F. Scott Fitzgerald
The Imposition – L. A. G. Strong
Turn About – William Faulkner
The Doll – J. Kessel
Reduced – Elizabeth Bowen
María Concepción – Katherine Anne Porter
The Cherry Feast – Ernst Glaeser
No More Trouble for Jedwick – Louis Paul
If You Can't Be Good, Be Cautious – T. O. Beachcroft
The Ball – Irène Némirovsky
Kneel to the Rising Sun – Erskine Caldwell
The Nowaks – Christopher Isherwood
Convalescence – Kay Boyle
The Station – H. E. Bates
Oklahoma Race Riot – Frances W. Prentice